A celebration of the amazing food & drink on our doorstep.
Featuring over 45 stunning recipes.

The Suffolk Cook Book

First edition printed in 2015 in the UK.

ISBN: 978-1-910863-02-2

Compiled by: Lisa Pullen

Written by: Kate Eddison

Photography by: Tim Green
www.timgreenphotographer.co.uk

Edited by: Rachel Heward, Phil Turner

Designed by: Paul Cocker

Cover art: Luke Prest, www.lukeprest.com

Contributors: Kelsie Marsden, Faye Bailey, Sarah Koriba, Kerre Chen

Thank you: Jimmy Doherty, Mick McCarthy & Ipswich Town FC, Martha Kearney

Published by Meze Publishing Limited

Unit 1 Beehive Works

Milton Street

Sheffield S3 7WL

web: www.mezepublishing.co.uk

Tel: 0114 275 7709

email: info@mezepublishing.co.uk

Printed by Bell & Bain Ltd, Glasgow

FOREWORD

Nature is my passion – it's been my obsession for as long as I can remember, but despite years of studying wildlife, I ended up working long days in a London office job, catching the tube home late at night, exhausted and craving fresh air instead of city smoke and dust. I yearned to get back to a more wholesome way of life. That's when I made the momentous decision to pack up my London life and embark on a big adventure.

I started my Suffolk farm 12 years ago with an aim to harness and put into practice some of the more traditional British farming methods to produce good quality, fresh, seasonal food as naturally as possible. I wanted to trade tasteless, pre-packed, mass-produced rubbish for real food, and get back to basics. And of course, get a bit of the 'good life' along the way. I think something in all of us wants to get back to nature and the pursuit of life's simple pleasures, whether it's growing your own vegetables or just walking barefoot along the beach.

Our restaurant on the farm uses only the best local, seasonal ingredients along with our own fresh, free-range, rare-breed meat and we have a team of chefs who work with our head chef to create some truly delicious dishes.

From pork, beef or lamb to breads, jams, preserves or ice creams, Suffolk has so much to offer when it comes to great produce. There are many world-class producers as well as some established family firms that have been producing some of the best food and drink for generations, and we stock a lot of their products in our farm shop.

It's so great to see local producers, shops and restaurants working together towards a common goal of putting great British food on the map, and I for one am happy to be a part of it.

Jimmy Doherty – Jimmy's Farm

CONTENTS

adidas
IPSWICH TOWN
FOOTBALL CLUB

Mick McCarthy's
BEEF STEW WITH YORKSHIRE PUDDING

Ipswich Town football manager Mick McCarthy's favourite winter warmer is his wife's classic beef stew. Using local ale and good-quality Suffolk beef, it is simple, hearty and full of flavour. Serves 4.

Ingredients

50g plain flour

1kg chuck or stewing beef, trimmed and cut into 5cm chunks

4 tbsp olive oil

2 onions, peeled and roughly chopped

500ml ale

250ml beef stock, or extra if needed

1 bay leaf

A few sprigs of fresh rosemary

2 carrots, cut into 5cm chunks

2 potatoes, cut into 5cm chunks

100g button mushrooms, halved if large

Salt and black pepper

For the Yorkshire puddings:

200g plain flour

3 eggs, lightly beaten

250ml milk

2 tbsp beef dripping

Salt and black pepper

Method

Season the flour with salt and pepper and spread it out on a plate. Dust the beef pieces in the flour to coat.

Heat a large saucepan or flameproof casserole dish over medium heat, add 2 tablespoons of the olive oil and start browning the beef, in batches, to seal on all sides. Remove the beef and set aside on a plate, adding the rest of the oil as you cook the remaining batches, if needed.

Add the onions to the pan and stir well with a wooden spoon, scraping up the browned bits from the bottom of the pan. Cook the onions for 5-10 minutes, until softened, then add the beef back in to the pan along with the ale, stock, bay leaf and rosemary. Bring to the boil, then reduce to a simmer, cover and cook for 2 hours, stirring occasionally. Add a little more stock, if needed, as it cooks.

Meanwhile, make the Yorkshire pudding batter. Put the flour in a large bowl and make a well in the centre. Add the eggs to the centre and begin beating into the flour, gradually adding the milk. Once all the milk is added, continue beating until smooth. Season with salt and pepper and set aside, covered, to rest.

After 2 hours of cooking, add the potatoes and carrots to the stew, give it a stir, replace the lid and cook for 30 minutes more. Add the mushrooms and cook for a final 30 minutes, until the beef is tender, the sauce is glossy and the carrots and mushrooms are soft. Remove the bay leaf and any stalks from the rosemary.

Meanwhile, preheat the oven to 250°C (fan 230°C). Divide the dripping between the holes of a 4-hole Yorkshire pudding tin or an 8-hole muffin tin. Place in the oven to melt and heat up. It needs to be very hot to make sure the Yorkshire puddings rise.

Give the batter a stir, then remove the hot tin from the oven and, working quickly and carefully, divide the batter between the holes. Place it back in the hot oven and immediately reduce the heat to 220°C (fan 200°C). Cook for about 20 minutes, until risen and golden.

Remove from the oven and serve immediately with the stew.

Friends around THE TABLE

In the centre of Woodbridge, The Anchor and The Table have hospitality covered. Simple food cooked well, excellent drinks and a consistently warm welcome await...

The hospitality industry runs in the Blackmore blood. With his family always running restaurants, pubs or cafés, Vernon Blackmore has never considered a different way of life. It's all about the satisfaction of seeing people enjoy a good meal or a nice drink for Vernon: "Life is so busy, if someone has a free half an hour to sit down and enjoy a beer and a sandwich or a couple of hours to savour a meal, there's nothing better than helping them enjoy that time."

A Woodbridge local, Vernon had been keen to open a pub for some time when he bought The Anchor in 2008. At the time, lots of traditional watering holes were disappearing from towns, and Vernon, passionate about proper pubs, wanted to keep the identity of the old pub and retain the feeling of a true 'local', while serving good food and equally good beers.

Situated on the quayside of the River Deben, the historic building is packed with old-world charm. Intimate rooms, dark wooden furniture, flagstone floors and roaring fires in winter, this is the perfect place to enjoy a Greene King cask ale after a walk along the river. In the back, the restaurant section embraces proper pub food Suffolk-style – Gressingham duck, Dingley Dell and Blythburgh pork, Simpers mussels, Springtide fish and Sutton Hoo chicken all feature on the menu. Simple food cooked well is the ethos here.

With one thriving business under his belt, Vernon leapt at the opportunity to open The Table when the premises became available nearby. The principles of excellent food and even better hospitality are the same as The Anchor, but this time it's a brasserie-style restaurant.

The characterful building and its Mediterranean-style courtyard make the ideal setting for light lunches accompanied by an interesting wine list and a broad selection of beers and soft drinks. A multitude of relaxed foodie events pepper the calendar, taking in the festival feeling over the summer months – Street Food Sundays showcase food from a particular country (think Mexican, Thai, Spanish or Cajun) accompanied by live music.

Both The Anchor and The Table are known for their friendly teams of staff, many of whom have been working there for years, and relaxed atmospheres. Whether it's a quiet drink or lunch in the sunshine, there's always a warm welcome in Woodbridge.

RESERVED
THE ANCHOR
IPA
the table

CARAMEL CHICKEN WINGS

with cracked black pepper

These Asian-inspired sweet and spicy wings are tender and succulent, and they make a popular starter or snack. Serves 2-4.

Ingredients

1 cup caster sugar

500g chicken wings

½ cup finely diced shallots

½ cup cracked black pepper

½ cup grated ginger

1 cup Squid brand fish sauce

A bunch of spring onions

1 red chilli, sliced for garnish

Method

Add the caster sugar to a heavy-bottomed saucepan, set over a medium-high heat and leave until it's an amber caramel. Watch it carefully so that it doesn't burn, as it can change very quickly, but do not stir it.

Whilst the sugar is caramelising, mix together the wings, shallots, cracked black pepper and ginger.

Once the sugar is amber in colour, reduce the heat and carefully add the fish sauce and stir together. Add the wings to the pan and stir thoroughly with the sauce. Cover with a lid and cook on a medium-low heat for 30 minutes or until the meat is falling off the bones.

Whilst the wings are cooking, slice the spring onions in half lengthways and then slice into thin strips. Place them in a bowl of ice-cold water and leave to curl.

Serve the wings with the sauce in a bowl and sprinkle with the spring onions and some sliced red chilli.

The Anchor
CREAMY SEAFOOD PIE

This English classic is just as satisfying whether it is served with garden peas or a simple salad. Serves 4-6.

Ingredients

For the mash topping:

5 large white potatoes, peeled

150ml double cream

100g butter

Salt and black pepper

For the filling:

500ml full-fat milk

2 bay leaves

200g fresh salmon, cut into large chunks

200g fresh cod fillet, cut into large chunks

100g smoked haddock, cut into large chunks

10 raw king prawns

1 white onion, finely diced

1 carrot, finely diced

2 cloves garlic, crushed

25g butter

1 tbsp plain flour

A pinch of saffron

50g mature cheddar, grated

A bunch of curly parsley, chopped

1 lemon

3 large eggs, soft-boiled

Salt and black pepper

Method

Start by preparing the potatoes for the mash topping. Put the peeled potatoes in a pan of cold water and bring to the boil. Simmer until tender.

Meanwhile, make the filling. In a large saucepan heat the milk with the bay leaves, add the fish and prawns and poach for 10-12 minutes.

While the fish is poaching, sweat the onion, carrot and garlic in a heavy saucepan until translucent. Add the butter and flour and stir to make a roux, then allow to cook out for 5 minutes.

Strain the fish and set aside, but keep the poaching liquor. Add the poaching liquor gradually to the roux along with the saffron, stirring well. Continue to cook over a medium heat until it starts to thicken, being careful it doesn't catch.

Add the grated cheddar and chopped parsley and remove the pan from the heat. Check the seasoning and add salt and pepper and lemon juice to taste. Carefully stir the poached fish and prawns into the sauce.

Heat the cream and butter for the mash topping in a saucepan. Strain the potatoes and mash using a ricer or potato masher. Whisk in the cream and butter and season with salt and pepper.

Preheat the grill. Spoon the filling into a deep oven dish and add the soft boiled eggs cut in half. Pipe the mash over the top and place under the hot grill until golden and crisp.

The Quay TO SUCCESS

A picture-perfect waterside location paired with perfectly executed bistro cooking has kept the locals and holiday-makers coming back to Bistro on the Quay year after year.

When Anthony and Kathy Brooks opened their bistro in 2002, it was the quayside charm of the historic old salt warehouses that attracted them to the area. Today, the Ipswich marina regeneration has seen a plethora of galleries, cafés, shops and hotels spring up around them, and their thriving restaurant sits at the heart of one of Ipswich's most delightful districts.

Although the setting with its undeniable natural beauty draws in tourists, this independent family-run restaurant remains an Ipswich favourite that has been welcoming regular diners for over a decade. Many loyal locals have been dining at Bistro on the Quay for such a long time that Anthony and Kathy count them amongst their close friends.

The hospitality shown by Kathy's front of house team is part of their winning formula for success, and many of the staff have worked at Bistro on the Quay for years. The dining room comes with a view into the open kitchen, so diners can enjoy watching their meals being expertly prepared by Anthony and his team. With 40 years of experience working as a chef, Anthony makes sure that everything is prepared from scratch in his kitchen, right down to the irresistible bread that is made fresh each morning. "My grandfather was a baker," explains Anthony, "so I've had my hands in the flour since the age of four".

This passion for serving the freshest and very best of produce means that Bistro on the Quay has a reputation for using the finest local ingredients, which are delivered daily. Locally caught fish is unsurprisingly their biggest seller during the spring and summer, while Suffolk game is popular during the autumn and winter.

"We aim to give everyone a reason to return", says Anthony who focuses on creating excellent fresh food, serving it in a welcoming environment and giving people fantastic value, from couples and solo diners enjoying a relaxed meal to big parties who can hire out the private room. The fixed price menu offers an attractive option for people to enjoy really good food at exceptional value and there is always something new to try at the ever-popular Tuesday Supper Special.

BISTRO
ON THE QUAY
Tel. 286677
BISTRO ON THE QUAY
BISTRO ON THE QUAY
BISTRO ON THE QUAY
BISTRO ON THE QUAY
BISTRO
ON THE QUAY

Bistro on the Quay

MONKFISH WRAPPED IN PARMA HAM

with roast ratatouille, basil mash and a Parmesan crisp

This is a practical, healthy and tasty recipe. It has just a few steps, all of which can be prepared hours in advance, which will hopefully allow you more time out of the kitchen with your friends and family. This recipe is also gluten-free. Serves 4.

Ingredients

For the monkfish:

600g monkfish fillet, cut into 4 even-sized pieces

8 slices Parma or Serrano ham

For the roast ratatouille:

1 aubergine, cut into 2.5-3cm pieces

1 clove garlic, finely chopped

1 small red onion, finely chopped

1 red pepper, cut into 2.5-3cm pieces

1 yellow pepper, cut into 2.5-3cm pieces

2 small courgettes, green or yellow, cut into 2.5-3cm pieces

A pinch of oregano

200g cherry vine plum tomatoes

Olive oil, for drizzling

Salt and black pepper

For the basil mash:

1kg Maris Piper potatoes, peeled and cut into chunks

A bunch of basil, roughly chopped

2 sprigs of parsley, roughly chopped

120ml olive oil

For the Parmesan crisps:

100g Parmesan cheese, finely grated

Method

Preheat the oven to 180°C.

Dry the monkfish fillets on kitchen roll, then roll each fillet up lengthways in two slices of ham, leaving the ends open. Refrigerate until needed.

For the ratatouille, place the aubergine, onion and garlic in a roasting tray, drizzle with olive oil, season and roast in the preheated oven for 10-12 minutes. Add the red and yellow peppers to the roasting tray, with more oil if necessary, mix together and roast for a further 10 minutes. Add the courgettes and oregano, mix together and cook for a further 5 minutes. Mix in the tomatoes, cook for another 4-5 minutes and check the seasoning. (If you are preparing in advance, stop the cooking process just after you add the tomatoes, then cool the mixture down until required.)

For the basil mash, simmer the potatoes gently in a large pan of salted water until tender. Pour into a colander and allow to drain fully. Put the herbs in a blender and liquidise with the olive oil until fairly smooth, then pass through a fine sieve into a suitable container. Mash the potatoes and add enough basil oil to moisten the mash and get the flavour of the basil. Check the seasoning and keep warm if serving now or cool the mash down until required. (Any leftover oil can be used later as a dressing.)

For the Parmesan crisps, line a baking sheet with baking parchment. Using a 6-7cm pastry cutter or ring as a guide, sprinkle the cheese inside the ring to form a thin layer. Remove the cutter and repeat 5-6 times. (This will give you a couple of spares.) Cook the Parmesan crisps in the middle of the preheated oven until the cheese is golden and starting to bubble. You may have to turn the tray to give an even bake. Remove from oven and allow to cool down before attempting to lift or loosen the crisps. They are best left on the tray somewhere cool until needed as they are easily broken.

When you are ready to serve, place some baking parchment on a roasting tray, sprinkle with a little olive oil then evenly space out the monkfish. Roast at the top of the preheated oven for 20-25 minutes or until the fish feels evenly firm. Reheat the ratatouille and microwave the basil mash until hot, stirring once. Place a spoon of mash and some ratatouille in the middle of a warm plate. Slice the monkfish into three rounds and place on top, drizzle with a little basil oil and finally stick a Parmesan crisp into the mash and serve.

Top Quality Tastes ON TAP

Proper pub food, seriously good beers and captivating premises, The Brewery Tap is one of Suffolk's most charming real ale pubs. Welcome to Ipswich's worst-kept secret...

When Mike Keen and his wife George opened The Brewery Tap in 2009, they knew they had their work cut out. Hidden away towards the industrial docks, most people living nearby didn't even know it existed. One look at the beguiling Gothic-looking building, though, and they couldn't resist trying to bring new life to its quirky walls.

Before he took over The Brewery Tap, the hospitality industry had taken Mike all over the world. After a 4-year HND, he worked as a general manager on cruise ships and lived in New Zealand, the USA and London, accruing valuable years of experience as a chef and in management. When he moved to Suffolk to work at Jimmy's Farm, he was immediately won over by the abundance of local produce available in the area and the exciting foodie vibe that permeated the entire region.

With such solid experience under his belt, Mike was just the man to make The Brewery Tap into something truly special. Putting good-quality regional food, real ales and local lagers at the core was the order of the day. You'll find only small beer producers on tap, most of which are local to the area.

Passionate about food, everything is made from scratch here, from pasta and Scotch eggs to puff pastry and ice cream. The kitchen is a place where traditional chef skills are embraced and nurtured.

The Brewery Tap's commitment to honest food has seen its reputation build up by word of mouth around Ipswich. The sausage rolls are nothing short of legendary now, and the regulars wax lyrical about the pickled eggs – the Marmite and Aspall cider pickled egg is one of the previous winners from the World Pickled Egg Championships after all!

It's a proper pub where people can come together from all walks of life and enjoy a beer, a chat and some classic British pub food cooked well. The beer gardens boast superb views, but you might just be happy watching the hens, ducks, quail and guineafowl pecking happily around the grounds. Set off the beaten track, its regulars have taken great pleasure in telling other Ipswich locals about their secret gem of a pub. However, with food, drink and an atmosphere this good, it was impossible to keep it a secret for long.

The Brewery Tap

A Warm Welcome AT THE INN

With the focus on friendly staff, cosy rooms and culinary excellence, it's no surprise that The Castle Inn has been listed in the Michelin guide for the sixth year in a row.

One glance at the menu at this historic inn and it's clear that husband and wife team, Tanya and Mark, are well-travelled foodies. From Korean pork to Risotto verde with samphire, flavour inspiration comes from around the world, while the produce remains resolutely local. After finishing college, Mark packed his chef's knives and his backpack and cooked his way around Australia, New Zealand, Spain, Italy, France, Thailand and Mexico. He met Tanya while working in the French Alps in 2000, and over the years that followed, they continued their travels, exploring the gastronomic delights on offer around the world.

After settling into city lives in London and establishing successful careers – Mark as a chef and Tanya in marketing – they stumbled across their dream business opportunity in the picturesque town of Bungay. A sleepy market town on the surface, Tanya and Mark discovered that there is a lot more to Bungay than meets the eye, and there has never been a dull moment since they took over the reins at this historic inn, which has been welcoming visitors since 1566.

Their ambition was to make The Castle Inn everything they would want to find in a country town inn, and it's fair to say they achieved that dream. Welcoming staff, a relaxed atmosphere, comfortable rooms, top-notch food and a great selection of beers always await here, and it's this winning combination that has led to praise in regional and national press, as well as making the inn a firm favourite with locals.

The cooking here is all about sourcing the best seasonal ingredients they can find – fresh fish from Lowestoft, Bantam eggs, locally reared meat from two neighbouring butchers and game from a traditional Suffolk supplier. With Baron Bigod brie from Fen Farm and vegetables, fruits and herbs supplied by individual growers (who swap their lovingly grown produce for a pint or a meal!), food doesn't get more local than this.

The Castle Inn
Comfy Bean bag cushions for outside benches.
Just relax

The Castle Inn

SALT MARSH LAMB SHOULDER WITH SAMPHIRE

This is a fabulous way to serve Suffolk lamb and samphire. Cooking lamb shoulder steaks slowly in this way gives succulent, tender results. Make sure you ask your butcher for bone-in shoulder steaks for the tastiest results. When samphire is out of season you could substitute curly kale or rainbow chard. Serves 4.

Ingredients

10g fresh rosemary leaves

2 cloves garlic, finely chopped

4 x 250g bone-in lamb shoulder steaks

A splash of olive oil

2 sticks celery, roughly chopped

1 small onion, chopped

250ml white wine

250ml water

1kg Maris Piper potatoes, peeled and sliced into ½cm thick slices

30g butter

300g samphire

Maldon sea salt and black pepper

Method

Preheat the oven to 200°C (180°C fan).

Rub the rosemary and chopped garlic into the lamb steaks, along with some salt and pepper. Heat the olive oil in a flameproof roasting pan (roughly 30cm x 30cm) on the hob, add the lamb and cook for 2 minutes over a medium heat on each side, until the meat is sealed and browned.

Add the chopped celery and onion, and cook for a further 4 minutes over a medium heat, stirring often, until the onions are transparent.

Add the white wine and water. This should be sufficient to immerse the lamb. Cover the lamb tightly with foil and transfer to the preheated oven for 1 hour. Check it regularly and top up with a little water if the stock reduces too much.

After 1 hour, arrange the sliced potatoes across the base of a separate buttered roasting pan. Add the lamb and juices, cover again with foil and cook for a further 45 minutes, or until the potatoes are soft. During this time, baste the lamb a couple of times to keep it moist.

Once the potatoes are cooked, remove from the oven and allow the dish to rest for 10 minutes before serving.

Whilst the meat is resting, heat the butter in a frying pan set over medium heat, add the samphire and sauté for 3 minutes or until tender. Serve the lamb on the potatoes topped with samphire.

Local lagers, reasonably-priced food and one of the best views in Ipswich, Cult Café Bar is the perfect place to watch the world go by.

Situated in one of University Campus Suffolk's buildings, a short walk from Ipswich's bustling quayside, the thriving Cult Café Bar is a student hot spot and local hub.

Mike and Georgie Keen jumped at the chance to take on this business when the opportunity arose in 2013. Already successfully running The Brewery Tap, they wanted to bring some of that winning formula to Cult Café by putting food and drinks at its heart.

You won't find any large-scale beer producers on tap. Instead you'll find seven draught lagers from small English brewers (mainly from East Anglia).

The menu, on the other hand, takes you around the world. Although the ingredients are sourced from as close to home as possible, the flavours are inspired by Mike's travels around the world with an irresistible street food vibe. From Cheju Jeju (Korean-style beef short ribs) to fat hot dogs and Canadian poutine, it's mouth-watering stuff. And despite the varied menu, it's all cooked on site – the burgers are hand-made and the chips are freshly cut in the kitchen.

With its handy location, it's a great base for students and staff of the university who can enjoy a 20% discount. Although this is by no means a student bar – with its big windows overlooking the marina, comfy sofas and laid-back atmosphere during the day, a real mix of people come to enjoy a lazy coffee or a reasonably priced lunch. In the afternoons, there is no better place to sip an English lager, nibble on a sharing platter and watch the boats come in. And by evening, why not hang around to watch one of the many great bands that play there?

Whatever time of day you visit, the feel in Cult Café Bar is relaxed and welcoming. It's obvious it's a happy place to work, visible from the quality of food coming out of the kitchen to the cheerful bar staff. Pop in and they'll be happy to tell you about what's coming up in the future, whether it's new craft beers on tap, upcoming festivals on the waterfront or the next live band to take the stage.

ower Ramparts
alifax & Belstead Rd.
proughton & Bramford
ramford & Sproughton
ramford & Claydon

Cult Café Bar

When Clare decided to turn her passion for cooking curries into a business, there was only one person she wanted to go into business with… her mum.

Clare Bennett-Smith has been cooking with her mum as long as she can remember. Growing up next door to her grandparents, she fondly remembers spending her childhood picking home-grown veggies and preparing them with her mother and grandmother. Watching and learning as the two generations of women before her transformed these goodies into dinner for the family, it's no surprise that this appreciation for good food stuck firmly in Clare's heart.

Whenever she would ask her mother, 'what did you put in this to make it so tasty?', her mother's answer was always the same: 'It's made with love.'

Thanks to a keen interest in travel, Clare's cooking was adventurous and exotic, and she found herself spending hours at a time in the kitchen creating delicious curries from scratch. Curries are our favourite food in the UK, yet so many people rely on flavourless sauces for a quick fix. Sure there must be a better way, Clare set her mind to creating something special… a spice kit that worked for today's busy curry-lovers, one that didn't rely on them chopping onions or ginger or garlic, and one that would pack a punch with authentic flavours.

She had her concept, now all she needed was a cooking partner – of course the only person she would turn to was her mum. Once they got started, there was no stopping this mother-daughter spice team, and in November 2011, Curry with Love was born.

From selling the initial eight kits at Bury St Edmunds market (with instructions printed on her home printer, neatly folded and painstakingly inserted into each pack!), they now have a booming business, rebranded packaging and an online shop with a range of 20 kits to buy.

With the hand-blended ground spices, whole spices, onions and garlic, the kits are a world away from the jars of sauce you'll find in the supermarket. Every mix is made with healthy eating in mind and all the cook needs to do is add meat, fish or veggies and some liquid (tomatoes or coconut milk usually) – no chopping, no mess, no fuss.

CURRY WITH LOVE
CHICKEN VINDAIL
NO CHOPPING, NO MESS, NO FUSS
SERVES 4
EST.
CURRY WITH LOVE
2011
THE AUTHENTIC CURRY KIT
PILAU RICE
EST. NET WEIGHT: 15G

SERVES 4
NO CHOPPING, NO MESS, NO FUSS
EST.
CURRY WITH LOVE
2011
THE AUTHENTIC CURRY KIT
CHICKEN VINDAIL
A FAIRLY HOT, TOMATO BASED CURRY
FROM SOUTHERN INDIA
HEAT
CURRY WITH LOVE
THE AUTHENTIC CURRY KIT
LENTILS WITH GARLIC & CHILLI
2011

Curry With Love

CHICKEN VINDAIL

with pilau cauliflower rice, lentils with garlic and chilli, and raita

Create an impressive meal with a little help from the amazing Curry with Love spice kits. Chicken vindail is a tomato-based South Indian curry and is often compared to a vindaloo. Don't worry, it's not as hot as a vindaloo, but it's wonderfully aromatic thanks to the distinctive flavours of star anise and cloves. For a low-carb alternative to rice, cauliflower is a firm favourite among foodies in the know – give it a try with the Curry with Love Pilau Rice Kit for a deliciously different side dish. Serves 4.

Ingredients

For the chicken vindail:

1 tbsp coconut or vegetable oil

1 Chicken Vindail Curry Kit from Curry with Love

800g skinless and boneless chicken thighs

400g tin of chopped tomatoes

100ml water

1 tsp white wine vinegar

Fresh coriander, chopped, to serve

For the lentils with garlic and chilli:

1 tbsp coconut or vegetable oil

1 Lentils with Garlic and Chilli Side Kit from Curry with Love

500ml water

250g cups dried split red lentils

A squeeze of lemon juice

For the raita:

250ml natural yoghurt

A small handful of fresh mint leaves, chopped

A squeeze of lemon juice

For the pilau cauliflower rice:

A large head of cauliflower, leaves removed

1 tbsp coconut or vegetable oil

1 Pilau Rice Kit from Curry with Love

Method

Start with chicken vindail. Heat the oil in a heavy-bottomed pan over a low heat. Add 'spice pack 1' from the Chicken Vindail Curry Kit and stir until fragrant. Add the chicken thighs and coat in the spices. Once the meat is sealed, add the chopped tomatoes, water, vinegar and 'spice pack 2' from the Chicken Vindail Curry Kit. Stir well. Once the curry starts to bubble, put the lid on and simmer over the lowest heat for about 1 hour, or until the meat is tender. Scatter over chopped coriander just before serving.

Meanwhile, make the lentils with garlic and chilli. Heat the oil in a pan over a low heat. Add 'spice pack 1' from the Lentils with Garlic and Chilli Side Kit and stir. When fragrant, add the water, lentils and 'spice pack 2' from the Lentils with Garlic and Chilli Side Kit. Stir well. Bring to the boil, then simmer on the lowest heat, uncovered, for 20 minutes, or until the lentils are soft. Add a squeeze of lemon juice before serving.

For the raita, place the yoghurt in a bowl and mix in the chopped mint leaves and lemon juice to taste. Set aside in the fridge until ready to serve.

Finally, make the pilau cauliflower rice. Grate the cauliflower (either in a food processor or by hand using the largest grater setting). Set aside until the chicken vindail and lentils are ready, as the cauliflower rice will take just a few minutes to cook.

Once the curry and lentils are cooked, add the oil to a large frying pan over a low heat. Add the spice pack from the Pilau Rice Kit and stir. Once fragrant, add the grated cauliflower and stir for a few minutes until the cauliflower is cooked through, but still has bite.

Serve the chicken vindail alongside the pilau cauliflower rice and lentils, topped with a spoonful of raita.

Living the GREEN LIFE

One of the most inspiring local food and farming ventures in Suffolk, Depden Farm Shop is bringing a taste of the good life to the local community.

It has been three years since Tim Freathy and his partner Mark Leadbeater opened Depden Farm Shop on their 6-acre smallholding. They had been living in this peaceful spot since 2005, balancing full-time jobs with rearing a few pigs, keeping some hens for eggs and growing vegetables. They chose to move here having grown increasingly concerned about how modern food was produced.

Selling his produce at local farmers markets was a side-line for Tim, and it wasn't until he was unexpectedly made redundant from his civil service position that he seized the opportunity to make his passion for good food and ethical farming the focus of his life – and he's never looked back.

The mission is simple – to bring the best local food to local people and to help us all learn new things, to live well and to tread a little lighter on the planet. For a relatively small plot of land, an incredible amount of things are going on.

The farm shop stocks their home-grown produce, and what they can't supply themselves they source from like-minded farms nearby. The philosophy is simple for Tim: "The food we sell is the food we like to eat." Meat comes in the form of Suffolk-raised pork and chicken, Cambridgeshire beef, and venison from just around the corner in Denham.

Mark is a physicist at Cambridge University, but before he goes to work every morning, he bakes all the cakes for the café and makes the chutneys, jams and preserves at the weekends. They also sell the best local cheeses, as well as some other English varieties from artisan producers. The bread is delivered every day – it has to travel only a couple of miles from the bakery, so you can always be sure of a fresh loaf!

As well as supper clubs, barbeques and a café, there is also a training centre, which has become a celebrated part of the community. Sign up for anything from cheese and wine tasting to how to keep pigs. They also provide training opportunities on the farm for people with learning disabilities through the Millennium Farm Trust.

The ethos is all about finding different ways to connect local people to food – as well as making sure people have fun at the same time!

GARDEN OF SUFFOLK
HAND MADE PRESERVES
Apricot
Jam
SUTTON HOO CHICKEN
SEASONAL GAME
DENHAM ESTATE VENISON

Depden Farm Shop

SUFFOLK BLUE & BROCCOLI TART

This tart always proves popular when served in the Depden Farm Shop Café. It is full of flavour from the delicious Suffolk Blue Cheese from Suffolk Farmhouse Cheeses. Serves 6.

Ingredients

For the pastry:

200g plain flour

A good pinch of salt

100g butter, chilled and cubed

About 4 tbsp cold water

For the filling:

2 tbsp olive oil

1 large onion, chopped

250g broccoli florets

4 eggs

150ml double cream

150ml milk

150g Suffolk Blue Cheese

Sea salt and freshly ground black pepper

Method

You will need a 10 inch loose-bottom tart tin or ceramic quiche dish.

To make the pastry, put the flour and salt in a food processor and whizz a couple of times to get air into the mixture. Add the chilled, cubed butter and blend until crumbly. Bind with cold water by adding a little at a time to the flour and butter mixture until it starts to from a ball in the machine – you may not need all of the water. It is important not to over process the pastry in the machine as this overworks the gluten in the flour and makes the pastry too elastic.

Remove the ball of pastry from the machine and knead gently, finally bringing it together into a smooth ball. Wrap in a plastic bag and chill in fridge for at least 30 minutes. The resting is important as it helps to relax the gluten in the flour. If you miss this step out, the pastry will not be as short and will shrink during cooking.

Preheat the oven to 200°C (fan 180°C).

Whilst your pastry is resting, prepare the filling. Heat the olive oil in a frying pan over medium heat, add the onion and fry until translucent but not coloured. Set aside.

Cook the broccoli pieces in a pan of salted boiling water until just cooked and retaining some bite. Drain and plunge the broccoli into the ice-cold water to halt the cooking and set aside.

Beat the eggs thoroughly, add the milk and cream and season with salt and black pepper. Mix well.

Roll out the pastry thinly and use it to line a 10 inch loose-bottomed tart tin or quiche dish. Prick the base of the pastry with a fork. Line it with a circle of baking parchment and fill with baking beans (in the absence of baking beans, left-over pastry works well). If you don't prick the pastry and weigh it down, it will balloon up during cooking and there will be no room for the filling.

Place the pastry in the preheated oven for 15 minutes. Remove the baking beans and place it back in the oven for a further 5 minutes to dry out the base. Baking the pastry case blind ensures that you don't get a soggy bottom. Not nice! Reduce the oven temperature to 180°C (fan 160°C).

To assemble the tart, scatter the onion and broccoli in the pastry case. Crumble in the cheese. Pour over the egg and cream mixture and bake in the oven for about 30 minutes. Check it after 25 minutes and give a bit longer if it's not cooked. The eggs should be set, risen and puffy with a light golden crust.

Elveden estate celebrates the finest local produce in the unspoilt East Anglia countryside.

Steeped in history, Elveden has been home to the Guinness family since 1894. Bought by Edward Cecil Guinness, the Earl of Iveagh, the business is today led by the fourth Earl of Iveagh, who keeps the family's heritage and their passion for food and farming at the heart of its ethos.

Set in stunning countryside, it's no surprise that there is estate-wide passion for rearing rare-breed animals, growing crops and protecting the flora and fauna of the local environment. Elveden estate grows such a fine selection of carrots, parsnips, onions and potatoes, they are supplied to supermarkets around the country, but there are rich pickings for the on-site restaurant, too, of course, where the field to plate philosophy is epitomised.

Step into the Courtyard restaurant or shops and you will see diners and shoppers enjoying the seasonal ingredients and local products at their best. Rare-breed lamb and beef dishes feature on the restaurant menu, often accompanied by home-grown and foraged ingredients from the estate. If that isn't enough to make your mouth water, step into the enticing food hall and stock up on the fresh vegetables, artisan cheeses and Elveden-recipe chutneys and jams that line the shelves.

The stunning converted restaurant building is sure to tick every box. It offers a light and airy dining space, which opens out on to the beautiful courtyard in summer for relaxed alfresco dining. However, in the winter, diners can enjoy a charming cosy atmosphere thanks to its warming wood burner.

The restaurant menu changes regularly to make the most of the freshest seasonal ingredients, and it includes plenty of tempting vegetarian options and gluten-free dishes. Every dish is cooked fresh to order from scratch, so the chefs will happily accommodate other dietary requirements, too.

Classic favourites are always popular, such as the Courtyard burger in a brioche bun with Estate Relish or locally-sourced fish and chips with homemade tartare sauce. Keep your eye on the specials board, which changes daily, for innovative dishes created by head chef Scott Taylor. He inspires his team to be creative with local ingredients and new techniques, so there is always something deliciously different on offer.

The restaurant is also celebrated for its afternoon teas, where diners can indulge in beautiful finger sandwiches, freshly baked scones and stunning patisseries, all created on the premises by the talented pastry chef. It's the perfect opportunity to savour a pot of loose-leaf tea or bottle of Champagne in unrivalled surroundings.

With such a plethora of dining options, a reputation for wildlife conservation and abundant charm, it's clear to see why Elveden is such a popular choice for those looking for a unique foodie day out.

DAMSON
ELVEDEN
ELVEDEN
www.elveden.com
Elveden Garden Gate
From Field to Fork
* Pea + basil soup with truffle bread £5.95
* Confit of duck leg, pan-fried pigeon breast with giroles £6.50
* Braised ox cheek with wholegrain mustard mash + seasonal vegetables £12.50
* Blackberry + frangipane tart + vanilla ice cream £5.95
ELVEDEN

Elveden

GLUTEN-FREE STICKY TOFFEE PUDDING

with Earl Grey ice cream

Sticky toffee pudding is a classic British dessert. It's complemented here by the ultimate sticky toffee sauce and a luxurious Earl Grey ice cream. At Elveden's Courtyard restaurant, head chef Scott Taylor hopes to ensure that there is something luxurious for everyone to enjoy, no matter what their dietary requirements. With this recipe at your fingertips, those who are gluten-intolerant will never have to miss out on indulgent desserts again. Serves 12.

Ingredients

For the Earl Grey ice cream:

250ml semi-skimmed milk

750ml double cream

2 Earl Grey tea bags

250g egg yolks

125g caster sugar

For the sticky toffee pudding:

400g dates, chopped

600ml water

4 tbsp bicarbonate of soda

2 Earl Grey tea bags

180g unsalted butter

340g dark brown sugar

2 tbsp golden syrup

2 tbsp black treacle

4 medium eggs

350g gluten-free flour

50g ground almonds

1 tbsp gluten-free baking powder

For the ultimate toffee sauce:

600g double cream

240g unsalted butter

240g dark brown sugar

50g black treacle

50g golden syrup

Method

Start by making the Earl Grey ice cream. Put the milk and cream in a pan with the tea bags and bring to the boil. Simmer for 25 minutes.

Meanwhile, mix the egg yolks and caster sugar with a wooden spoon until combined (do not use a whisk otherwise it will be too frothy).

Add the hot milk mixture to the egg yolk mixture, stirring gently in a figure-of-eight motion. Strain through a fine sieve (this will catch the tea bags too) into a clean thick-bottomed pan. Continue to stir over a low heat (do not allow this mixture to boil or you will end up with expensive scrambled egg!) until it coats the back of the spoon.

Allow to cool, then place in the fridge to chill. Once chilled, either churn the mixture in an ice cream machine or transfer to a Tupperware container and put in the freezer, whisking it every 15-20 minutes until firm.

To make the sticky toffee pudding, preheat the oven to 180°C (160°C fan).

Put the dates, water, bicarbonate of soda and tea bags in a pan, bring to the boil and boil for 15 minutes. Remove and discard the tea bags and allow to cool a little, then blend in a food processor or blender and set aside to cool completely.

Meanwhile, whisk the butter and dark brown sugar together until creamy, then add the golden syrup and treacle. While whisking slowly, add the eggs, one at a time. Fold in the gluten-free flour, ground almonds and gluten-free baking powder, using a figure-of-eight motion with a spoon. Fold in the date mixture in the same way, until completely smooth.

Line an 8 x 6 inch cake tin with greaseproof paper, pour in the batter and bake in a preheated oven for 45 minutes, or until a knife comes away cleanly when inserted into the centre.

Meanwhile, make the ultimate toffee sauce. Place all of the ingredients into a thick-bottomed pan and bring to the boil over a medium heat, stirring occasionally. Once it has reached boiling point, the sauce is ready. As it cools, the sauce will thicken.

Serve the sticky toffee pudding warm from the oven (or reheat the following day), drizzled with the sauce and accompanied by the Earl Grey ice cream.

Taking the REINS

A real ale pub with on-site brewery, eco campsite and superb food, the new landlord at The Edwardstone White Horse Inn is putting this historic pub at the heart of the community.

Mick Fallon has been in the pub business all his life. It's a career that has taken him all over the country, but the charm of rural Constable country eventually led him to Suffolk. In fact, it was his partner June Ash, who initially suggested they look for a pub with a campsite, and when they stumbled upon the Edwardstone White Horse Inn in its idyllic surroundings, they were immediately won over.

Mick is passionate about good pubs and firmly believes the local pub should be a focal point for the community. As the inn is in a rural location, it relies on the reputation of its food to draw people in. With fabulously talented head chef Benjamin Newman (or Jamin as he's known) in the kitchen, this isn't a problem for The White Horse Inn. His menu is based around local ingredients and he always includes the beef and pork from neighbouring farms – the pork comes from a farm about seven miles up the road and the beef from a farm just five miles away.

It's no surprise that The White Horse has a Green Tourism award under their belt. The eco-friendly ethos runs through everything they do and they are always looking for the next way to stay green. The plan for the future is to grow as many of their own vegetables, greens and salad leaves as possible in their gardens. Their focus is on getting the best ingredients from as close to home as possible and transforming them into deliciously satisfying food.

With the award-winning Mill Green Brewery on site, situated in an old stable, the pub always has their real ales on tap, as well as an ever-changing selection of guest ales from carefully selected breweries. It's an ale-drinker's paradise at the Edwardstone White House Inn, and it's the commitment to keeping the beer selection as exceptional as the food menu that keeps the regulars coming back.

For those visiting the area, a peaceful campsite and two self-catering cottages are the ideal base to explore the splendid countryside. Keep an eye on their calendar too – from beer festivals to folk nights, there's always something happening at The Edwardstone White Horse Inn.

Edwardstone White Horse
THE WHITE HORSE INN.
MILL GREEN BREWERY
BREWED ON SITE
WHITE HORSE BITTER 3.6% £3-00
MASSACHUSETTS 3.2% 3-10
CHINOOK 4% £3-30
SIMCOE 4% £3-30
MICK'S YORKSHIRE BEST 4.2% £3-40
WIFI: df4dc4d6ee
THE WHITE HORSE INN.
Add onion rings @ 90p.
Spent Malt
PIG
HENNY RARE BREED 9 MILES AWAY
COW
only 4 miles away
Malted Barley (often grown organically in chelsworth
Malt
Mill Green Brewery
Beer
White Horse Inn
Happy People
* All food is cooked fresh to order there will be a wait during busy periods.
MILL GREEN BREWERY

Edwardstone White Horse

PULL A PIG APART

This is a celebration of the pig with ham hock croquettes, slow-cooked pork belly, crackling pencils, fennel-crusted pork cutlets and smoked pancetta. Start this recipe a day in advance. Serves 10.

Ingredients

For the ham hock croquettes:

2kg smoked ham hock

1 tbsp coriander seeds

1 tbsp black peppercorns

3 bay leaves

4 tbsp finely chopped parsley

2 tbsp wholegrain mustard

Flour, beaten egg and panko breadcrumbs, for coating

oil, for deep-frying

For the pork belly:

1 pint of Suffolk cider

2 tbsp fennel seeds

A piece of pork belly, about 3kg (ask the butcher to remove the skin and bone)

Salt and pepper

For the potatoes:

1kg potatoes, peeled and diced

150g butter

1 bunch of spring onions, finely chopped

For the carrot purée:

25g butter

300g carrots, peeled and diced

2 star anise

2 sprigs of fresh tarragon

100ml chicken stock

50ml double cream

For the apple ketchup:

500g Granny Smith apples, peeled and diced

80g caster sugar

Seeds of 1 vanilla pod

50ml cider vinegar

For the fennel-crusted pork cutlets:

2 tbsp fennel seeds

1 tbsp pink peppercorns

100g soft light brown sugar

150g pork cutlets

For the Savoy cabbage:

150g diced smoked pancetta

½ Savoy cabbage, finely shredded

A knob of butter

For the liver:

1kg pig's liver

A knob of butter

½ tsp fresh thyme

Method

Start with the ham hocks. Put the ham hocks in a large pan and cover with water. Bring to the boil and skim off the residue. Lower the heat to a simmer and add the coriander seeds, black peppercorns and bay leaves. Cook for 4 hours until the meat falls off the bone. Strain, setting the stock aside for later and allow to cool. Strip all the meat from the bone and put into a bowl, removing all the fat. Add the parsley and mustard.

Put 2 pints of the reserved stock in a pan. Bring to the boil then simmer until reduced by half. Add to the meat and mix well. Lay out some cling film and make a long sausage of the meat mixture using the cling film as a skin, compacting it firmly. This should be the diameter of a 10 pence coin. Put it in the fridge to chill and set for 2 hours.

The next day, for the pork belly, preheat the oven to 150°C. Put the cider and fennel seeds into a large roasting tin. Pat dry the skin of the pork, score it and season. Place it in the tin, cover with foil and cook in the preheated oven for 3 hours 30 minutes. Allow to cool, then place in the fridge for 3 hours to set when cool enough.

Once set, preheat the oven to 200°C. Remove the skin and scrape away all the fat. Cut the skin into long strips and place between two sheets of greaseproof paper on a tray with another tray on top. Roast for 20 minutes to create crackling pencils.

Run the diced potatoes under water to remove the starch. Boil in a pan of lightly salted water until tender. Mash the potatoes then add the butter, finely diced spring onions and seasoning. Keep warm.

For the carrot purée, heat the butter in the pan, add the carrots and cook for 2-3 minutes. Add the star anise, fresh tarragon and chicken stock, and simmer until soft, then add the double cream. Blitz to a purée and season. Set aside.

For the apple ketchup, put the apple, sugar, vanilla seeds, cider vinegar and 50ml water in a pan and cook until soft. Transfer to a blender or food processor and blitz to a purée. Set aside.

For the fennel crust, place the fennel seeds, pink peppercorns, sugar, salt and pepper in a grinder and blitz. Alternatively, bash to a powder in a pestle and mortar. Set aside.

When ready to serve, preheat the oven to 185°C. Sear the pork cutlet on both sides in a hot pan. Dip in the herb crust and place in the preheated oven for 6 minutes with the pork belly.

Heat the pancetta in a separate pan until caramelised. Add the finely shredded Savoy and sweat until softened. Add the butter and season. Keep warm.

Heat the oil for deep-frying in a deep-fryer or heavy-bottomed pan. Cut a 1½ inch piece from the ham hock sausage. Dip it in the flour, then the beaten egg and then roll in panko breadcrumbs. Deep-fry for 90 seconds. Drain on kitchen roll.

Season the liver and sear on both sides in a hot pan. Add the butter and thyme.

For each plate, place a good dollop of apple ketchup on the plate and spread across to form a canal. Add the croquette to the plate. Add a good spoonful of mash and place the liver on top. Place the pork belly on the plate with a crackling pencil. Add the savoy and place the cutlet on top. Finish with a few dollops of carrot purée.

The Best of
BRITISH BEEF

Set on 190 acres of idyllic landscape, Emmerdale Farm Shop is a traditional family business that is being embraced by modern food-lovers.

Since they bought the farm 12 years ago, Jeremy and Wendy Thickitt, with help from their children Richard and Charlotte, have been gradually expanding their family-run farm shop, much to the delight of the local community.

The Thickitt family have seen a real resurgence in the demand for high-quality meat, with people being increasingly interested in where their meat comes from.

They rear a variety of traditional British cattle breeds, from the famous Suffolk Red Poll to Aberdeen Angus, Hereford, Belted Galloway and Shorthorn. The cattle graze on the verdant fields and marshes by the river during the summer and are reared slowly to guarantee the best flavour.

In the butchery, customers can see the meat hanging behind glass panels. Watch in awe as the skilled butchers mince the meat and turn it into the freshest burgers or their deliciously succulent meatballs, which are a firm favourite with the regulars. Sausages are also made on the premises, all in front of your eyes with local meat and selective seasonings. If you're in luck, you'll be around for one of the daily sausage tastings!

As well as their own beef, they also stock locally reared free-range pork, lamb, poultry and game. With a wealth of knowledge about meat, the friendly team are able to answer any questions about provenance and cuts. Particularly passionate about those underrated cheaper cuts of meat, the butchers here will happily explain the best cooking techniques for getting the best out of them.

A family affair, Wendy's sister Zoe runs the Red Poll Tea Room, serving up hearty breakfasts, irresistible cakes and light lunches. Jeremy's wife Wendy can usually be found in the farm shop, accompanied by their daughter. Perfect for picking up just about anything you need, the shop stocks everything from seasonal vegetables and locally produced dairy to frozen foods and store-cupboard essentials. Don't leave without grabbing one of their famous homemade pies – they sell out fast.

Emmerdale Farm Shop

Emmerdale Farm Shop
EASY MEATBALLS

Meatballs are a firm favourite with our customers, but they are simple to make yourself at home. Pop in to the shop for some fresh mince and whip these up in no time. The mixture of beef and pork provides fabulous flavour, and you can just use a store-bought tomato sauce if you don't have time to make one. Perfect for a quick mid-week meal. Serves 2-3.

Ingredients

225g minced chuck steak, Red Poll if available

225g minced pork shoulder, free-range if available

2 eggs

50g breadcrumbs

2 tbsp grated Parmesan

1 heaped tbsp finely chopped fresh (or dried) basil

2 cloves garlic, finely chopped

1 tsp salt

1 tsp black pepper

500g tomato sauce (either homemade or store-bought)

Method

In a large bowl mix the mince, eggs, breadcrumbs, Parmesan, basil, garlic, salt and pepper together.

When well mixed, divide the mixture into 6 even portions and shape them into palm-sized meatballs. If time allows, place them in the fridge, covered, for 30 minutes. This will allow them to become firmer and let the flavours develop.

Preheat the oven to 200°C (180°C fan).

Place the meatballs in an ovenproof dish and pour over the tomato sauce. Place a lid on top or cover with foil and cook the meatballs in the preheated oven for 45-55 minutes, removing the lid or foil after the first 30 minutes of cooking.

Streets AHEAD

Friday Street Farm Shop has everything you'd expect from a traditional British farm shop, and a whole lot more to boot...

Set against the ever-beautiful backdrop of the Suffolk countryside, James Blyth's traditional arable farm has gradually expanded into a flourishing foodie destination, set between the quintessentially English seaside towns of Aldeburgh and Southwold. The impressive farm shop has shelves stocked with goodies from local suppliers and artisan producers, selling everything you could need – from fresh meat, vegetables, cheese and eggs to store-cupboard basics, gifts, pet food and gardening supplies.

Taking over the reins five years ago, James has been responding to local demand for high-quality meat and seasonal vegetables, and business is booming. From spring to winter, he makes the most of the fertile land to produce fine crops. We're talking asparagus without the air miles and potatoes fresh from the field. Or if you fancy doing the picking yourself, pop along to pick your own luscious ripe strawberries when they're in season.

For meat-lovers, the butchery is a real boon to the area. Master butcher Ian Manthorpe maintains the exceptional standards for which Friday Street Farm Shop has become renowned to offer the highest-quality meat. Customers travel from far and wide for his knowledgeable advice on breeds, cuts and cooking, not to mention his traditional friendly service.

The 60-seater restaurant is the jewel in the crown. With a focus on wholesome good cooking using vegetables straight from the farm and meat from the on-site butchery, locals and holiday-makers come together to enjoy hearty breakfasts, light lunches and indulgent puds.

The cottage pie is a top-seller. It showcases freshly minced beef from the butchery, which is topped by creamy mashed potatoes – from the farm of course! Ingredients certainly don't have to travel far around here before they're whipped up into delectable dishes.

Nobody can leave without trying one of the famous home-made puddings, lovingly baked on the premises. Check the blackboard to see what's on offer each day, as it will depend on what ingredients cooks Claire and Sarah have at their disposal that day. One thing you can be sure of though, these legendary desserts always keep the locals coming back for more!

F
FRIDAY STREET
FARM SHOP
Picnic
Spot
Friday Street Farm Shop
FRIDAY STREET
BUTCHERY
CAFÉ
RESTAURANT
SERVING COFFEES, LUNCHES
& AFTERNOON TEAS
OPEN DAILY

Friday Street Farm Shop

RASPBERRY ROULADE

When there is a glut of raspberries at Friday Street Farm, this is the ideal dessert to use them in. It's a firm favourite in the café and a great choice to make at home using local fresh and store-cupboard ingredients from the farm shop. Serves 8-10.

Ingredients

2 tsp cornflour

2 tsp white wine vinegar

2 tsp vanilla extract

6 egg whites

300g caster sugar

A handful of flaked almonds

500ml double cream

2 punnets of home-grown Friday Street raspberries

Method

Preheat the oven to 170°C (fan 150°C). Line a baking tray with baking parchment.

Mix the cornflour, white wine vinegar and vanilla extract together. In a mixing bowl, whip the egg whites to stiff peaks. Pour the cornflour mixture and sugar slowly into the egg whites and mix together.

Spread the mixture out on to the lined baking tray. Sprinkle the flaked almonds evenly across the mixture.

Bake in the preheated oven for about 45 minutes until golden and slightly crisp to touch.

Allow to cool on the baking tray, then turn upside down onto a sheet of baking parchment.

Whip the double cream and spread it evenly over the meringue. Sprinkle the raspberries onto the cream and then carefully roll the meringue up, using the baking parchment to help you.

Thirty Years of GREATNESS

Overlooking the picturesque market square in Lavenham, The Great House offers an exceptional fine dining experience to match its magnificent setting.

Housed in a simply stunning 14th-century building, The Great House is the jewel in the crown of Lavenham's beautiful medieval village. It has a fascinating history and a long line of illustrious owners. Regis and Martine Crepy bought this piece of Suffolk history in 1985, transforming it into a renowned French restaurant.

They added the five luxurious bedrooms a year later, carefully balancing the décor to retain the historical charm of the building while offering every modern comfort.

The reputation for excellence in both food and service is recognised across Suffolk and the UK, and this is a prime destination for a foodie break as well as a hot spot for locals. Countless accolades reward their consistent quality and service – currently listed 26th in Square Meal's top 100 UK restaurants, listed in Harden's top 100 restaurants in the UK, winner of the Editor's Choice Gourmet Award in the 2015 Good Hotel Guide, named the AA Inspector's Choice 2015 for Restaurant with Rooms with three AA rosettes, and winner of the inaugural Fabulous Food Award in Alistair Sawday's 2015 British Hotel Guide.

Service is effortless yet impeccable under the watchful eye of manager Thierry Pennec who has worked with Regis for 16 years. There is a tremendously loyal team of staff, some have been with the Crepys for over 20 years and have an exceptional working relationship. They all share the same passion for good food and wine and are as dedicated to ensuring that their guests are superbly looked after and have a memorable time.

It's impossible not to feel at ease as soon as soon as you walk in. The glassware sparkles on the pristine white table linens and flickering candles provide a relaxed atmosphere. Whether guests are dining al fresco on the pretty patio in summer or enjoying the cosy open fire in winter, the ambience of The Great House is hard to beat.

Choose from the à la carte menu or opt for one of the excellent value set lunch and dinner menus. It's all based on classic French cooking. Never one to be concerned with changing fashions, Regis places the emphasis on balancing flavours and letting his top-quality ingredients shine. Talented head chef Enrique Bilbault has worked with Regis for 26 years and it's clear this partnership is a winning formula.

They use the best local suppliers they can where possible for the freshest meat and fish. As you'd expect from a quality French restaurant, their legendary cheese trolley contains over 30 French cheeses sourced from the Rungis Market in Paris, as well as local Norfolk and Suffolk cheeses from Hamish Johnston Fine Cheeses.

The wine list boasts over 350 fantastic new and old-world vintages, and also gives customers the opportunity to taste some lesser known wines, keeping the list fairly priced. If you fancy a little fizz, the Great House's own label Champagne is perfect for celebrations.

They are no strangers to special events – fundraisers for local charities have been a successful part of the 30th birthday celebrations in 2015, as well as the popular wine tastings, which are held regularly.

Being highly praised by local and national media, The Great House is always welcoming new guests. However, they are particularly proud of their loyal regulars, some of whom first ate there as children. It's a pleasure for the Crepys to see these guests returning with their own children, introducing them to one of life's simple pleasures – great food.

LAVENHAM
SUFFOLK
THE GREAT HOUSE
RESTAURANT & HOTEL

The Great House

BAKED HALF-SHELL SCOTTISH QUEENIES

"Carbonara" glazed with buffalo mozzarella, coriander, chilli and tomato butter sauce

Using the finest scallops is essential for the best results in this recipe. The distinctive and creative flavour combination mixes a carbonara-style sauce with a hint of chilli, aromatic coriander, creamy mozzarella and melting tomato butter. Serves 4.

Ingredients

5 vine tomatoes, peeled, quartered and deseeded (seeds, pulp and juices reserved)

2 tsp extra virgin olive oil

A pinch of Maldon salt

A pinch of caster sugar

250g salted butter

20g fresh coriander, finely chopped

1 fresh Thai chilli, deseeded and finely chopped

1 banana shallot, finely chopped

100g smoked streaky bacon, finely diced

500g fresh chestnut mushrooms, finely chopped

50ml medium white wine

100ml whipping cream

32 half-shell fresh queenie scallops

150g buffalo mozzarella, diced into 32 cubes

32 micro coriander leaves

Salt and black pepper

Method

Start by making the tomato butter. Pass the reserved tomato pulp, seeds and juice through a fine sieve and keep the juice.

Heat the olive oil in a saucepan, add the quartered tomatoes and cook to a purée consistency. Add the reserved juice, Maldon salt and caster sugar, and simmer until reduced by half. Put in the fridge.

Cut the butter in cubes and whip with an electric beater until it forms a white and foamy consistency. Add the coriander, chilli and the cooled tomato purée. Mix well.

On a work surface, layer three sheets of cling film on top of each other, making sure there are no air bubbles between each sheet. Place the tomato butter on the cling film and roll it up into a sausage. Put the butter in the fridge to set.

Meanwhile, make the carbonara. In a saucepan, sweat the shallot and streaky bacon. Add the mushrooms and cook together until any liquid has evaporated. Add the white wine, simmer until reduced by half and add the cream to finish. Season to taste, then set aside.

Preheat the oven to 200°C (fan 180°C).

Place eight half queenies on each plate. Add one-third of a teaspoon of the carbonara mix on each half queenie, a cube of mozzarella and a thin slice of tomato butter on top.

Put the plates in the preheated oven for 3 minutes until the butter is melted and the queenie is still soft and moist. Add a micro leaf to each queenie to decorate. Bon appetit!

The Great House
ROASTED FILLET OF MUNTJAC

with heather honey and fig sauce

Muntjac, one of the smallest varieties of wild deer, was introduced to the UK from China. Here it is paired simply with a few flavours to keep the venison as the star of the plate – use the finest heather honey you can for the best taste. Serves 4.

Ingredients

1 tsp coarse sea salt

4 x 150g boned fillets of muntjac venison

20g salted butter, plus a knob of butter for frying

2 tbsp heather honey

Juice of 1 lemon

4 fresh figs, cleaned and cut in half

100ml venison stock

A few sprigs of chervil

Method

Preheat the oven to 200°C (fan 180°C).

Trim some of the fat off the venison fillets. Put the sea salt in an ovenproof frying pan with a knob of butter and set it over a high heat. Place the venison fillets in the pan for 1 minute turning them over to seal on both sides.

Put the fillets in the preheated oven for 5 minutes. Once the fillets are cooked, place on a warm plate covering them with another plate upside down.

Remove the fat from the pan and melt the butter with 1 tablespoon of the honey, half the lemon juice and the halved figs. Place over medium heat for 2 minutes, then remove the figs from the pan and set aside.

Put the rest of the honey and lemon juice in the pan with 20ml of water and the venison stock. Let it reduce for 2 minutes.

Slice the venison fillets to your liking and place them on individual plates. Return the figs to the pan for 1 minute. Cover the venison fillets with the sauce (or serve the sauce on the side, if you like) and add the figs. Decorate with a sprig of chervil on top.

The Great House
STRAWBERRY & MASCARPONE

chilled soup with mint

This elegant dessert is simple to make at home and is the perfect recipe to use up a glut of summer strawberries. Serves 4.

Ingredients

450g ripe strawberries, hulled

25g granulated sugar

Juice of 1 lemon

125ml red wine

1 tbsp balsamic vinegar

A few sprigs of fresh mint, thinly sliced, plus extra for decoration

200ml whipping cream

30g icing sugar

Seeds from ½ vanilla pod

100g mascarpone cheese

To serve:

Blackberries, strawberries, red currants and blueberries

Method

Put 250g of the strawberries in a pan with the sugar and lemon juice. Cook gently over a low heat for 2–3 minutes, until the sugar has dissolved. Pour everything into a blender and blitz to a purée.

Transfer the strawberry purée to a large bowl and then set aside to cool. When the soup is cool, stir in the red wine, balsamic vinegar and mint. Cut the remaining strawberries into quarters and add them to the soup.

Whip the cream in a bowl with the icing sugar and vanilla seeds, then fold it gently into the mascarpone.

Ladle the soup into four shallow soup plates or glass bowls. Soak a soup spoon in hot water, then dip it into the mascarpone mixture to make an oval 'quenelle' and place one on top of each bowl of soup. Decorate with berries and sprigs of fresh mint and serve immediately. Bon Appetit!

The Remarkable DUCK PEOPLE

In the stunning countryside of East Anglia, 'the Duck People' at Gressingham Duck® are passionate about their unique breed.

When it comes to ducks, they certainly know a thing or two... Did you know that only female ducks quack? It seems that there is nothing they can't tell us about ducks, and with such a wealth of knowledge and expertise at the core of the business, you can rest assured that they are committed to top-quality produce. For the tastiest duck, they believe the birds must have the best rearing, and this commitment to quality has always been the key to their success.

Miriam and Maurice Buchanan began their company in 1971 and started rearing Gressingham Ducks® in Suffolk in 1989. A true family venture, it is run today by their sons, William and Geoff, but Maurice and Miriam can't tear themselves away from their beloved business, and they still live in a bungalow on the farm, where they remain at the heart of daily activity.

The Gressingham Duck® first came about when the small but flavourful wild mallard was crossed with the larger Pekin duck, giving a meaty, succulent breed with more breast meat, less fat and a rich gamey flavour. With such an impressive array of qualities, you can see why this special breed has gained such popularity.

Every Gressingham Duck® is raised on one of their Red Tractor assured farms in East Anglia, and it's this dedication to rearing healthy birds that gives the duck its superior culinary qualities. It's healthier than you may think, too – a skinless duck breast has half the calories and less than half the fat of a skinless chicken breast. Although all that flavoursome fat that is released from under the skin is a real winner for making the most delicious roast potatoes!

It goes without saying that many of us love to tuck into duck. It's consistently popular in restaurants, yet some lack the confidence to cook it in their own kitchens, so Gressingham Duck® have embarked on a campaign to get more of us cooking duck at home. Think crispy legs, succulent breasts and luscious whole roasted ducks... From aromatic Asian seasonings to classic fruity flavour pairings, the team at Gressingham Duck® will have us all whipping up delicious duck dishes in no time.

Gressingham

Gressingham Duck®

FIVE-SPICE DUCK LEG

with Asian slaw

This recipe is very simple to prepare and the end result is a delicious summery dish. It uses the kitchen cupboard staple Chinese five-spice powder, which is sprinkled over the legs before placing in the oven. Instead of serving the whole duck legs on top of the Asian slaw, you could try shredding the duck and serving it in a tortilla wrap with the slaw. Serves 2.

Ingredients

For the duck:

2 Gressingham Duck® legs

1 tsp five spice

Salt and pepper

For the Asian slaw:

1 carrot, peeled and grated

½ small red cabbage, cored and grated

1 mini red pepper and 1 mini yellow pepper, deseeded and finely sliced (or 1 large pepper of either colour)

½ small onion, finely sliced

1 clove garlic, finely chopped

2cm piece root ginger, peeled and finely chopped

Grated zest and juice of 1 lime

1 tsp sesame oil

2 tsp fish sauce

2 tbsp toasted sesame seeds

Salt and pepper

Method

Preheat the oven to 180°C (160°C fan).

Prick the skin of the Gressingham Duck® legs with a fork or cocktail stick, then season well with the five-spice powder and some salt and pepper.

Place the duck legs skin-side up on a baking tray with a rack. Cook in the preheated oven for 1 hour-1 hour 15 minutes until tender.

Meanwhile, prepare all the vegetables for the slaw by placing the carrot, red cabbage, peppers, onion and garlic in a large mixing bowl.

When the duck is ready, remove it from the oven and cover with foil.

Add the ginger, lime zest and juice, sesame oil, fish sauce and toasted sesame seeds to the mixing bowl with the vegetables. Season with salt and pepper and then toss everything together well.

Divide the slaw between two plates, place a duck leg on top of each portion and serve.

Gressingham Duck®

HONEY, ORANGE & THYME-GLAZED

Duck breast

This sweet and fruity recipe showcases the classic flavour pairing of rich Gressingham Duck® breasts and citrusy, juicy oranges. Ideal for a quick and tasty supper, this makes a fantastic meal for two. Serves 2.

Ingredients

10 new potatoes

2 large oranges

2 Gressingham Duck® breasts

100g honey

2 cloves garlic, finely chopped

½ bunch thyme

1 tsp orange marmalade

Salt

Method

Preheat the oven to 180°C (fan 160°C).

Bring a pan of salted water to the boil, add the new potatoes and cook until tender. Drain and, when cool enough to handle, cut the potatoes in half. Set aside.

Meanwhile, peel and segment one of the oranges. Slice off the top and bottom of the orange with a sharp knife, then place the flat bottom of the orange on a chopping board and use the knife to slice off the peel from top to bottom all around. Remove any remaining pith, then carefully slice between the membranes to cut out the segments of orange flesh. Set the segments aside.

Grate the zest from the other orange, then squeeze out the juice. Set aside.

Score the skin of the duck breasts with a sharp knife and pat with kitchen roll to absorb any excess moisture.

Place a dry frying pan over a low-medium heat, season the duck breasts with salt and place into the pan skin-side down. Cook for 6-8 minutes until the skin is crisp and golden. Pour off any excess fat as you cook. Flip the breasts over and cook for 30 seconds to seal the other side.

Transfer the duck breasts to a baking tray skin-side up and cook in the preheated oven for 4 minutes.

Meanwhile, place the frying pan back over the heat and add the orange zest and juice, honey, marmalade, garlic and half the thyme. Cook, stirring occasionally, until the sauce is reduced by half.

Add the cooked and halved potatoes and the orange segments, and continue to simmer until loosely sticky. Remove from the heat and set aside.

Remove the duck from the oven and glaze the skin generously with some of the sauce. Return to the oven for a 2-3 minutes for rare, or cook for slightly longer if you prefer it medium to well done.

Remove from the oven and allow the duck breasts to rest for at least 5 minutes.

When you are ready to serve, divide the sauce and potatoes between two plates. Carve the duck breasts into five or six pieces and place on top. Scatter the remaining thyme leaves on top and serve with your favourite greens.

Gressingham Duck®

ROAST DUCK

with honey and rosemary jus and roast potatoes

One of Gressingham's favourite dishes, this recipe makes use of the tasty fat from the duck to make delicious roast potatoes that are light and fluffy on the inside and crispy on the outside. Gressingham Duck® fat is available to buy, but you can save the fat from your roast duck for next time you make roast potatoes. The richness of the duck is complemented by the sweet rosemary and honey jus. Serves 4-6.

Ingredients

1 whole Gressingham Duck®

4 tbsp Gressingham Duck® fat

1kg roasting potatoes, peeled and chopped into large chunks

4 sprigs fresh rosemary

1 onion, roughly chopped

1 garlic bulb

250ml white wine

400ml chicken stock or water

50g butter

3 tbsp honey, plus extra to taste if needed

Salt and pepper

Method

Preheat the oven to 200°C (fan 180°C).

Remove any giblets from inside the duck (you can use these for making stock, if you like) and weigh the duck to calculate the cooking time. Pat the skin dry with kitchen roll and pierce the skin around the legs using a skewer. Season the duck with salt and pepper.

Place the duck on a trivet in a baking tray big enough to allow you to fit the potatoes around the edge. Add the Gressingham Duck® fat.

Place the duck into the preheated oven and calculate the cooking time (20 minutes per 500g plus 20 minutes extra). After the first 45 minutes, add the potatoes to the baking tray, baste with the duck fat and add the rosemary, onion and garlic. Season with a generous amount of salt and place back in the oven. Every half an hour, turn and baste the potatoes with the duck fat.

When the duck is cooked, remove it from the oven, cover with foil and set aside to rest. Remove the potatoes, baste with more duck fat and place back in the oven until crisp and cooked. Remove the potatoes from the tray and keep warm.

Carefully pour off any remaining fat from the baking tray into a heatproof bowl and save for another time. (Allow to cool to room temperature, then cover and store in the fridge.)

You should now be left with just the duck juices, garlic, rosemary and onion in the baking tray. Place the baking tray over a low heat on the hob and add the wine. Bring to the boil and use a wooden spoon to scrape the bits off the bottom of the tray. Strain into a clean pan, add the chicken stock or water and cook over medium heat until reduced by half or until it starts to thicken. Stir in the butter and honey. Taste for seasoning and sweetness and adjust accordingly with extra salt, pepper or honey.

Serve the roast duck with the roast potatoes and the jus.

A Truly English EXPERIENCE

Charm and elegance remain at the heart of the quintessentially English Harriets Café Tearooms, which has been treating customers to home-cooked food in Bury St Edmunds since 1999.

It's impossible to miss the huge pillars that mark the entrance to Harriets Café Tearooms in the heart of beautiful Bury St Edmunds. This Grade II listed building was once home to the fire station, which explains the stunning high ceilings – at one time a practicality for the fire engines to fit inside, today adorned with spectacular chandeliers that glisten in the light and airy space.

Although there are now three branches of Harriets, with Cambridge and Norwich too, the original tearoom in Bury St Edmunds is where the business began. However the story of Harriets starts much further back in time, with the stories that Harriet's grandmother Mary used to tell of trips to the Lyons Corner Houses in London, where she enjoyed the cakes and tea and was utterly captivated by the smartly dressed 'nippies' darting around.

The old English charm that encapsulated these tales stayed with Harriet into adulthood. She wanted to bring back that feel of exceptional service, but most of all she wanted to establish a tearoom where the focus was on home-cooked food and old-fashioned family values.

There is no question that she achieved just that. From approaching the building, every little detail is considered – an immaculate entrance, a warm welcome and beautiful décor. A world away from modern cafés, guests are shown to their tables and handed menus by smartly dressed waitresses.

The top-notch training is evident – the staff know Harriets inside out and can answer any question whether it's about specific ingredients or the name of the distinctive wallpaper pattern!

This is a venue where the customer is the focus, and this is the key to their success. In the rush of modern life, what a joy it is to step back in time in a tranquil setting and enjoy a treat from a bygone era. Savour a cup of tea and a scone, a light lunch, a hearty breakfast or a lavish afternoon tea in attractive surroundings, with staff who go above and beyond to make each and every visit a truly memorable one.

Harriets Café Tearooms

Harriets Café Tearooms

BELGIAN TRIPLE CHOCOLATE BROWNIE

An ever-popular choice on the menu at our Tearooms, made using the finest Belgian chocolate our rich and indulgent brownies are the ultimate chocoholic's delight. A treat for yourself and your loved ones you will be sure to wow at any dinner party. Why not warm through and serve with vanilla pod ice cream and a drizzle of tangy raspberry coulis? Serves 8.

Ingredients

4 free-range eggs

500g caster sugar

110g plain flour, sifted

150g cocoa powder, sifted

250g unsalted butter, plus extra for greasing

80g mixed Belgian milk, dark and white chocolate callets (or chips)

Method

Grease a 12 inch rectangular baking tin with butter. Preheat the oven to 170°C (fan 150°C).

Separate the egg whites from the yolks. Put the egg whites in a large bowl and whip until stiff. Beat the egg yolks and sugar together in a separate bowl, then carefully fold them into the egg whites.

Gently fold in the sifted flour and cocoa powder.

Melt the butter in a pan set over a medium heat and add to your mixture. Combine everything together.

Stir through all of the desired Belgian chocolate callets.

Transfer the mixture into the greased baking tin so the mixture is around 1 inch deep. Cover with foil and put the brownie in the preheated oven for 30 minutes.

Carefully remove the foil and reduce the oven temperature to 160°C (fan 140°C). Place the brownie back in the oven for another 15-25 minutes until cooked through. To check, gently pierce the brownie in the centre with a sharp knife or skewer to see if any uncooked mixture remains.

Allow the brownie to cool for 45 minutes at room temperature before carefully cutting the edge and turning out.

Spilling the BEANS

Champions of home-grown pulses and grains, Hodmedod is reintroducing us to traditional British staple foods and developing the production of new crops – and they have some fabulously original ideas for what to do with them.

Nick Saltmarsh, Josiah Meldrum and William Hudson founded Hodmedod in 2012 in order to bring home-grown fava beans (small seeded dried broad beans) back to British kitchens. These tasty and nutritious pulses have been grown in Britain since the Iron Age and were once an important part of our diet. Today, they are overlooked in the UK, with most of the British crop going to Egypt.

Having cooked the beans themselves to make delicious houmous, falafels, ful medames, soups and curries, Nick, Josiah and William set out to see if there was a wider appetite for them. On behalf of local organisation East Anglia Food Link they packed a tonne of beans at William's kitchen table and distributed them through community groups and local shops. Each pack contained a postcard with a short questionnaire on the back to collect feedback on the beans.

Not only are fava beans delicious and nutritious, they're also environmentally and agriculturally beneficial, playing an important role in farming rotations, requiring less water than other crops, improving the soil and providing food for bees. The split beans are easy to cook too, as they don't need soaking. Unsurprisingly, the response to the trial packs was overwhelmingly positive. Hodmedod was born and has been building sales of British fava beans and expanding its range of pulses and grains ever since.

Nick, Josiah and William are continually on the lookout for other less well-known foods that can be grown on British farms. Among Hodmedod's most popular products are "Black Badger" carlin peas and quinoa from the plains of Essex.

As well as the dried products, Hodmedod also offers a range of canned pulses and roasted beans and peas. The aim is to have us all filling our cupboards with these versatile, protein-packed products, celebrating forgotten British food heroes and discovering new British crops for a more sustainable future.

And what is a hodmedod anyway? Debate around this old East Anglian dialect word rages between Suffolk and Norfolk – depending on who you're talking to it might be a hedgehog, snail, ammonite or even a curl of hair. What these meanings have in common is that they're all small and round, just like the ancient beans, peas and grains Hodmedod is bringing back to our kitchens.

Split Dried
500g
www.hodmedods.co.uk
Hodmedod's
GREAT BRITISH
beans

Hodmedod's FAVA BEAN HOUMOUS

Split dried fava beans make a delicious alternative to chickpeas as the basis for houmous, with the great advantage that they don't need soaking and cook down to a creamy consistency without the need for a food processor. This fava bean houmous can be cooked from scratch in just 30 minutes. Hodmedod's fava beans are all grown on British farms, making this houmous lower in food miles too. For an even more British houmous, try substituting cold-pressed rapeseed oil for the olive oil and hazelnut paste for tahini. Serves 4.

Ingredients

100g Hodmedod's Split Dried Fava Beans

2 tbsp tahini

2 tbsp olive oil, plus extra for drizzling

2 tbsp lemon juice

½ tsp mild dried chilli

½ tsp grated lemon zest

1 tbsp chopped parsley and/or mint, plus extra to garnish

1 small clove garlic, crushed and finely chopped

Smoked paprika, to garnish

Method

Put the fava beans in a saucepan with plenty of water. Bring to the boil and simmer for 30 minutes. (After 30 minutes cooking, the beans will be soft and creamy but will largely be still intact with some bite – this will give a coarse houmous. For a smoother consistency, cook for 40 minutes in just enough water, topping up if necessary, and the beans will cook down to a more consistently creamy paste.)

Meanwhile, mix together the tahini, olive oil and lemon juice, stirring well for a creamy consistency. Add the mild dried chilli, lemon zest, and chopped parsley and/or mint. Add the crushed and finely chopped garlic.

When the beans are cooked, drain, place in a bowl and stir in the tahini dressing. Drizzle with a little more olive oil and garnish with chopped parsley and smoked paprika.

Hodmedod's CARLIN PEA & GINGER

gluten-free chocolate cake

When Lindsey Dickson, who writes about food on her blog The Eating Tree, gave us this recipe we were concerned that it might be rather dry and earthy, and, well, taste of peas. Nothing could be further than the truth and this cake has quickly become a Hodmedod favourite. The ginger and chocolate combine with the peas to make a moist, rich cake which is not overly sweet. Easy to make, beautiful to look at and an extremely good keeper, need we go on? The recipe makes a large cake that will cut into 12 servings easily, making it excellent for entertaining. Like most chocolate cakes, it is even better the next day, so, for best results, make the cake the day before, wrap in foil overnight and decorate the following day. Serves 12.

Ingredients

For the cake:

200g good-quality dark chocolate or chocolate chips

175g unsalted butter, plus extra for greasing

4 pieces of stem ginger, chopped (about 80g)

3 tbsp syrup from the jar of stem ginger

200g cooked Hodmedod's Carlin Peas (or canned Hodmedod's Carlin Peas are an excellent alternative if you don't have time to soak and cook dry peas)

200g light muscovado sugar

1½ tsp ground ginger

4 eggs, separated

Cocoa powder, for dusting

For the decoration:

125g good-quality dark chocolate

80ml double cream

20g unsalted butter

2 tbsp of syrup from the jar of stem ginger

1-2 pieces of stem ginger, chopped

Method

Grease a 9 inch spring-release cake tin with butter and line the bottom with baking paper. Dust the sides with cocoa powder.

Preheat the oven to 185°C (fan 165°C).

Break up the chocolate and put it in a heatproof bowl with the butter and ginger syrup.

Put the bowl over a saucepan of gently simmering water and stir occasionally until melted. Do not let the bottom of the bowl come into contact with the simmering water.

Put the peas into a food processor and process until resembling coarse ground almonds.

Add the sugar, ground ginger and egg yolks to the pea mix and process again until combined. Turn the mixture out into a large bowl and stir in the chopped ginger.

In a separate clean bowl, whisk the four egg whites until stiff.

Stir the melted chocolate, butter and ginger syrup into the pea, ginger, egg yolk and sugar mix. Using a metal spoon, gently fold half the egg whites into the chocolate mixture, then fold in the remaining half.

Pour the mixture into the prepared cake tin and cook in the preheated oven for 45-50 minutes until set. Don't worry if the cake cracks slightly.

Remove from the oven and leave to cool on a wire rack for 10 minutes before taking off the outer ring.

When the cake is completely cool, make the chocolate covering. Put the chocolate, cream, butter and ginger syrup in a heatproof bowl set over gently simmering water and stir until melted, smooth and glossy. Do not let the bottom of the bowl come into contact with the simmering water.

Spoon the chocolate over the top of the cake and spread to the edges with a palette knife. Leave to set a little before distributing the remaining pieces of ginger on the top.

When cutting, wipe the knife blade between cuts to ensure a beautifully clean cut.

Food Fresh from THE FARM

With a plethora of TV appearances, books and high-profile food campaigns surrounding his name, Jimmy Doherty is Britain's most famous pig farmer.

You'd be forgiven for assuming that life is all PR and personality for this charismatic countryside champion, but the focus for Jimmy Doherty has always been, and always will be, on farming and food.

At Jimmy's Farm, good farming and good food go hand in hand. It all started with pigs for Jimmy and, although the farm shop now boasts an impressive array of rare-breed beef, lamb and chicken, it's still the pig that steals the show around here. The selection of pork, bacon and gammon is a delight to behold, not to mention Jimmy's famous sausages.

The restaurant, housed in a lovingly restored 200-year-old converted barn, lures diners in with its stunning timber beams and airy interior. The atmosphere is cheerful and relaxed, a perfect place for families to take a break from their activities around the farm and indulge in some of its bounty.

But a glance at the seasonally changing menu tells you this is no traditional farm café. Friendly staff serve up show-stopping dishes, with a focus on the pork that started it all – go for proper pulled pork, served in a brioche bun with apple sauce, slow-roast pork doughnut, crispy pig's cheek and black pudding, or share a rare-breed pork platter for a taste of it all. This really is a pork-lover's paradise.

Head chef Jon Gay prides himself on putting local food at the forefront of his menu. His inspirational approach to using the best local and seasonal ingredients (with vegetables and herbs from the farm garden, of course!) mingles with the no-nonsense approach to food that Jimmy, alongside his celebrity pal Jamie Oliver, has become famous for. And the result is truly tasty, honest fare that lets its Suffolk heritage shine.

Jimmy's Farm ROAST PORK

with crackling and apple ketchup

You can't beat roast pork with crackling. It's all down to buying a really good piece of meat, then all the flavour will be there already and most of the work is done for you. This simple recipe for apple ketchup is just the thing to serve with it, and so easy to make you'll wonder why you ever bought apple sauce in a jar! Serves 6.

Ingredients

For the pork:

A loin of pork, about 2.5kg

2 tsp Aspall white wine vinegar

A bunch of fresh thyme

A few bay leaves

Pink, white and black peppercorns

Maldon sea salt

For the apple ketchup:

400g cooking apples, peeled and cored

1 whole vanilla pod

200g caster sugar

Juice of 1 lemon

175ml Aspall white wine vinegar

Method

Preheat the oven to 220°C (fan 200°C).

Firstly score the pork skin with a really sharp knife, or even a Stanley knife if you have a clean one! Make straight cuts just though the skin, in the same direction you will be carving, but be careful not to cut all the way through the skin.

Massage the 2 tsp vinegar into the pork skin, before rubbing in some sea salt and the leaves from the fresh thyme, bay leaves and peppercorns.

Roast in the preheated oven for 25 minutes, before turning down the temperature to 190°C (fan 170°C) and continue cooking for a further 2 hours 30 minutes. Let the pork rest for at least 40 minutes before carving.

To make the ketchup, slice the apples finely and place in a saucepan. Slice the vanilla pod in half lengthways and use the knife to scrape out the seeds. Add these to the pan along with the sugar, lemon juice and vinegar. Bring to the boil and boil for 10 minutes.

Once the apples are soft, strain the liquid into a jug and place the apple mix into a blender or food processor. Begin blending until a thick apple purée is formed. Gradually add the reserved liquid into the blender until the mixture is a smooth, spreadable apple ketchup. Refrigerate before serving. The ketchup will last for up to 4 weeks in the fridge.

Modern FRENCH FLAIR

Maison Bleue in Bury St Edmunds is famed for its understated elegance, sophisticated surroundings and modern French cooking, winning critical acclaim both locally and nationally.

Set within a deep-windowed heritage building, Maison Bleue offers a relaxed and welcoming ambience. Subtle pastel tones, classic décor, period features and tables swathed in crisp white linen with delicate glasses and carefully chosen flowers provide the perfect setting for lunch, dinner or larger groups in the elegant private dining room. First impressions are taken seriously here by husband and wife owners Pascal and Karine Canevet and no detail is overlooked.

Established in 1998, this highly celebrated restaurant doesn't need to shout about its myriad awards. With Trip Advisor reviews placing it among the UK's top 10 fine-dining restaurants, it's their commitment to the quality of each and every individual dining experience that makes this such a special place to visit.

Expertly managing front of house, Karine exudes natural grace and professionalism. She hand-picks her team from the best French catering schools, such is her commitment to exceptional standards. "Presentation is key," she explains, "we do the very best to ensure that the restaurant is the perfect setting to enhance Pascal's creative dishes."

To complement the food, Karine and her team offer recommendations from their extensive wine list, which includes a great selection, ranging from classic old-world wines to some notable new-world choices. The wine cellar boasts over 300 finest vintages, personally selected by Karine and Pascal.

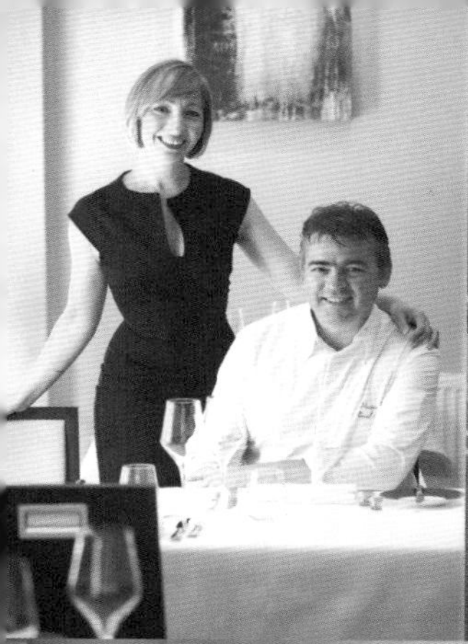

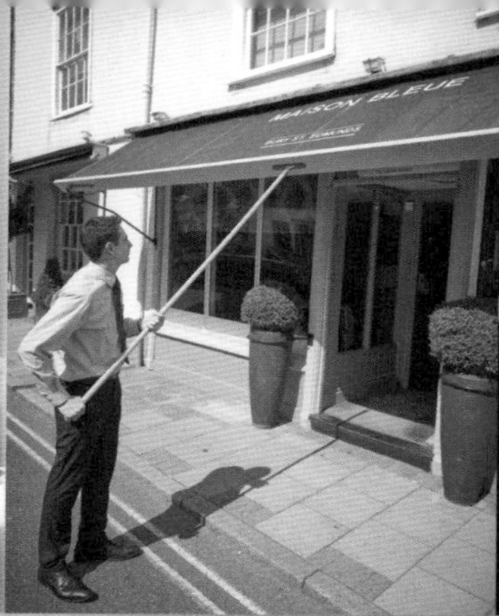
MAISON BLEUE

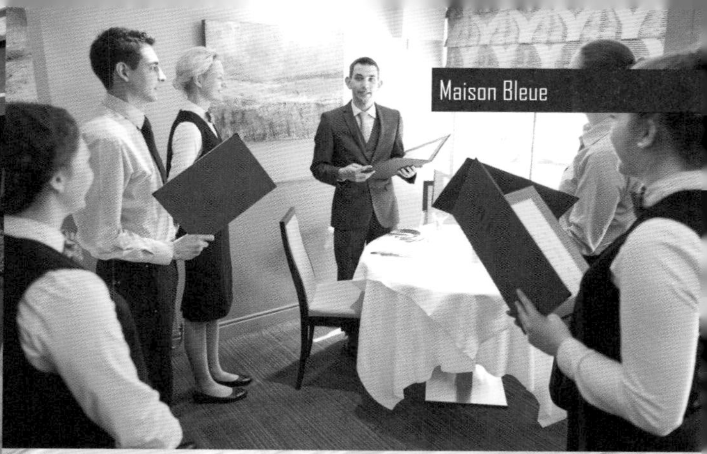

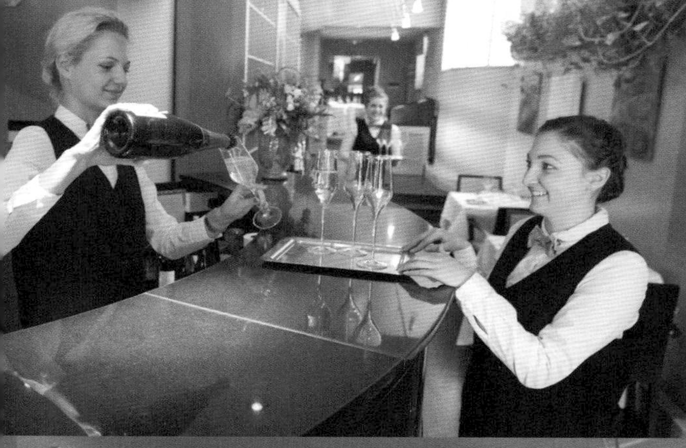

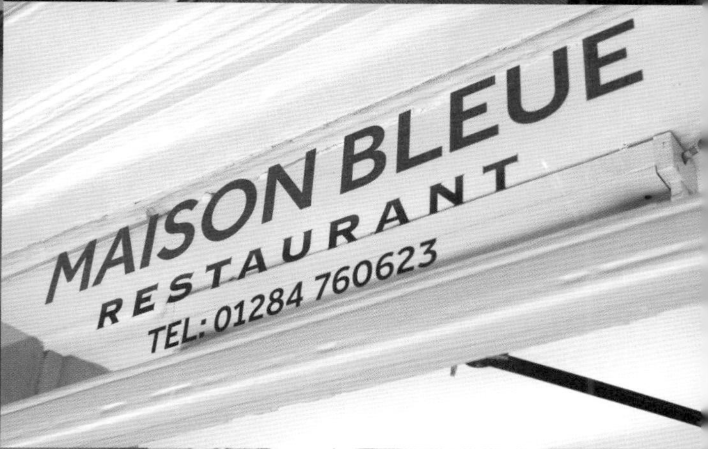
MAISON BLEUE
RESTAURANT
TEL: 01284 760623

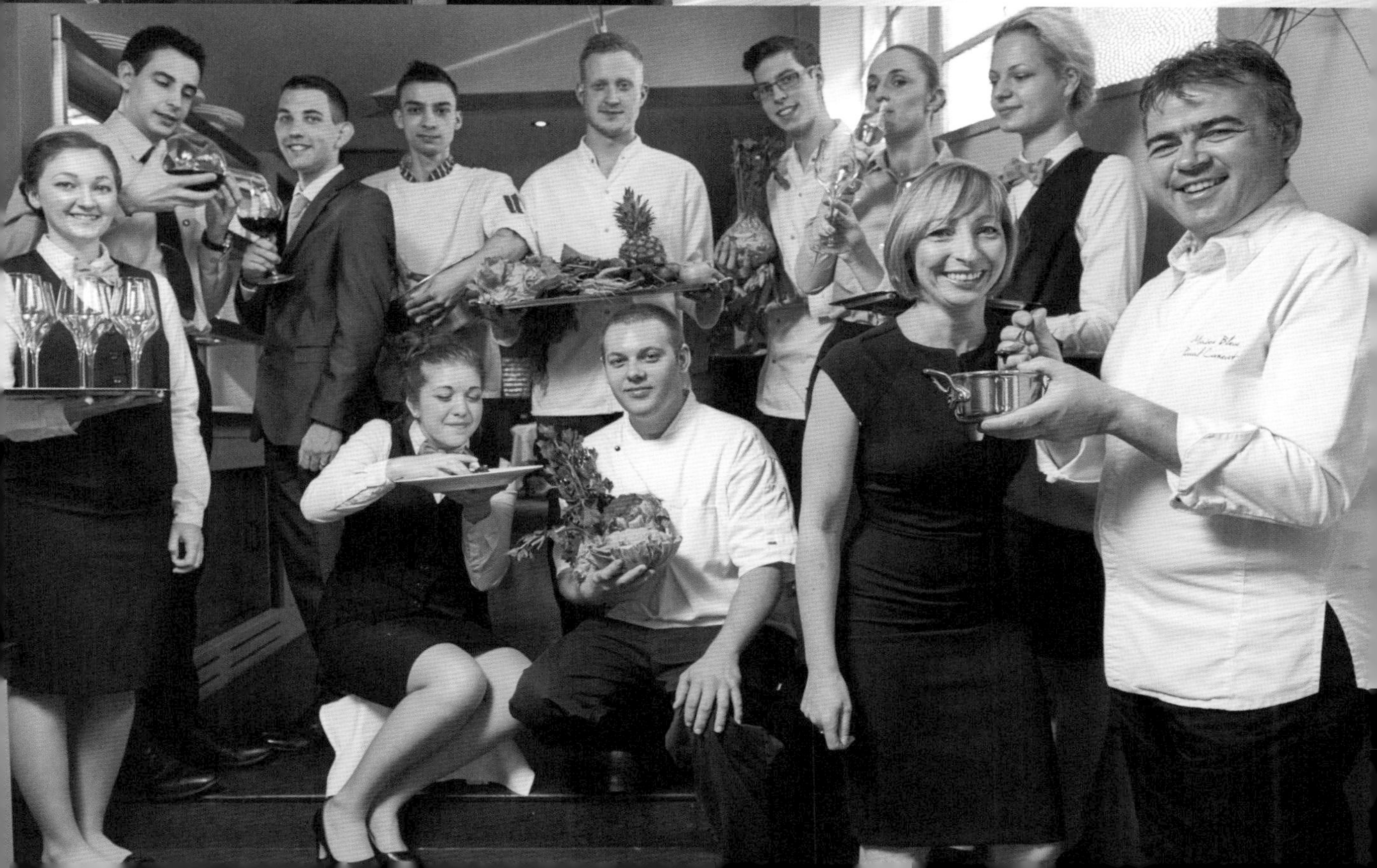

In the kitchen, Brittany-born head chef Pascal is responsible for the highly praised seasonal menus. Lunch and à la carte menu change frequently with unique innovative twists on classic dishes. Presenting his food beautifully on the plate comes naturally to Pascal, and his creative dishes will not fail to delight. However, for Pascal, there is much more to fine dining than aesthetics. "Of course I'm creative and love presenting food beautifully, but the delicate balance of flavour is what I'm all about."

Whilst the style of his cooking has evolved over the years, receiving many awards and accolades along the way, the fundamental backbone of Pascal's dishes remains unchanged. Impeccable seasonal ingredients with distinctive and imaginative twists are beautifully cooked and brought together on the plate, unmistakeably celebrating all things Suffolk.

Pascal's passion for the finest French modern cooking is rivalled only by his commitment to seasonal, local ingredients; a philosophy he inherited from his mother who instilled in him a love of home-grown produce. From the vegetables and herbs to the fish, meat and cheese, Pascal ensures he knows the provenance of his ingredients. Building up good relationships with suppliers is key and he will often be found visiting local farms from where he buys his produce. Perhaps it's this genuine delight he embodies for food that makes his menu stand out above that of his rivals.

Active members of the community, the list of Pascal and Karine's charitable commitments is extensive to say the least. Suffolk Breakthrough Breast Cancer, Sir Bobby Robson's Foundation, St Nicholas Hospice, Focus 12 and Each to name a few, are amongst the charities supported by Maison Bleue.

Suffice to say, Bury St Edmunds is dear to the hearts of this charming husband and wife team; and with their unwavering passion for supporting the community, championing local produce and delivering culinary excellence, they have put Bury St Edmunds firmly on the gastronomic map.

Maison Bleue
CORNISH SARDINES

A stunning seafood dish with a subtle balance of flavours and a pop of red beetroot makes a colourful starter. Choose high-quality fresh sardines from your local fishmonger – the fresher the better. Serves 4.

Ingredients

1 cooked beetroot

50ml balsamic vinegar

24 sardines with tails, scaled and butterflied

15g shallots, finely chopped

100g mascarpone

10g flat leaf parsley, finely chopped

2 feuilles de brick (thin sheets of French pastry, available in large supermarkets and online)

A knob of salted butter, melted, for brushing

6 small heirloom tomatoes

Extra virgin olive oil, for drizzling

Candied baby beetroots, sliced, to garnish

Salt and black pepper

Method

Place the cooked beetroot in a food processor or blender, add the balsamic vinegar and blitz. Season with salt and pepper, then set aside until needed.

Roll 16 butterflied sardines and secure with a toothpick. Refrigerate until needed.

Sweat the shallots in a pan for 4-5 minutes over medium heat until softened. Cut the rest of the sardines into small cubes and place into the pan with the shallots. Cook for 3 minutes, then remove from the heat.

Transfer the sardine and shallot mixture to a medium bowl and add the mascarpone and chopped parsley. Using a wooden spoon, work it until smooth. Season to taste. Using a spatula, scoop the mixture into a piping bag. Chill in the fridge for at least 2 hours.

Preheat the oven to 150°C (fan 130°C).

Cut both feuilles de brick into eight 5cm x 10cm strips (you should have 16 strips altogether) and brush them with melted salted butter. Roll the strips around stainless-steel pastry tubes and place into the preheated oven for about 4 minutes, until they have coloured. Remove from oven and set aside to cool on the pastry tubes. Once cooled, remove the stainless-steel tubes and fill the pastry with the chilled sardine and mascarpone mixture.

Increase the oven temperature to 250°C (fan 230°C).

Place the 16 rolled butterflied sardines in the preheated oven for 2 minutes until cooked.

Blanch, peel, quarter and deseed the heirloom tomatoes. Season with salt and pepper, and drizzle with extra virgin olive oil.

Divide the sardine fillets and rolls between 4 serving plates and add the heirloom tomatoes. Drop some spots of beetroot dressing onto different areas of the plate and garnish with sliced and seasoned baby candied beetroot. Enjoy!

Maison Bleue

CREEDY CARVER DUCK

A delicious roasted breast and stuffed leg ballotine, served with chicken liver velouté and jus. This dish is full of flavour. Serves 4.

Ingredients

100g chicken breast

1 egg white

120ml whipping cream

70g Suffolk chorizo, diced

1 whole free-range Creedy Carver duck, deboned but with the skin left on

20g shallots, finely chopped

70g butter, plus extra for pan-frying

100g chicken livers

10ml brandy

100g broad beans

20g Girolles mushrooms

Salt and black pepper

For the jus:

1 duck carcass (ask your butcher for this when he has deboned the duck)

1 large carrot, roughly chopped

1 celery, roughly chopped

Leek trimmings

2 cloves garlic, lightly crushed

1 bouquet garni

Zest of 1 orange

6 peppercorns

2½ pints water

Salt

For quality and taste, we use Creedy Carver duck, as they are grown in welfare-friendly conditions. Ask your butcher to debone the duck for you, leaving the skin on. Ask for the carcass too, which you will need for the jus. Start this recipe a day ahead.

Method

To make the ballotine, chop the chicken breast roughly and place in a food processor. Pulse until finely chopped. Add the egg white and a little salt and pepper. Blitz on full speed for 3 minutes, stopping the machine twice to scrape down the sides. While blitzing, incorporate 100ml of the cream in a steady stream and purée until smooth. Scrape the mixture into a large bowl and add the diced chorizo and stir.

Lay out the boneless legs of duck (skin-side down) on a sheet of cling film. Season with salt and pepper. Spread out the chicken stuffing all over the meat. Roll the stuffed duck into a neat sausage shape using the cling film, and twist the cling film at each end to tighten and seal. Steam in a steam oven at 60°C for 8 hours. (You can also do this in a bain-marie in a domestic oven.)

To make the chicken liver velouté, place the shallots and the 70g butter in a medium pan set over a medium heat. Add the livers and sauté until browned on both sides, but still medium rare; about 2 minutes on each side.

Deglaze the pan with the brandy, scraping up the bits on the bottom of the pan. Cook just until all the liquid has evaporated. Do not let the livers start to stick to the bottom of the pan. Transfer the livers and shallots into a food processor and turn it on.

After the livers have been spinning for about 1 minute, slowly add the remaining 20ml cream and blend until smooth. Season to taste. Transfer to a bowl, cover and store in the fridge until needed.

To make the duck jus, preheat the oven to 220°C (fan 200°C).

Put the broken duck carcass, carrots, celery, leek and garlic in a flameproof roasting pan and place in the preheated oven to brown and slightly caramelise for 25 minutes. Place the carcass and vegetables, along with the bouquet garni, orange zest and peppercorns into a large pan. Put the roasting pan over a medium heat on the hob and deglaze it with a little of the water, using a wooden spoon to get off all the nice burnt bits. Add this to the pan with the rest of the water. Bring steadily to the boil and simmer for around 2 hours.

Pass the stock through a fine sieve into a bowl. Season and let it cool, then skim any fat that would have risen to the top. Place the stock into a clean pan and bring to a simmer. Cook until it has reduced by about three-quarters.

To cook the breasts, preheat the oven to 200°C (fan 180°C).

Score the skin of the duck breasts with a sharp knife and season with salt and pepper. Place the duck breasts skin-side down in a large frying pan set over a medium heat. Colour the skin, for 10 minutes, pouring off the excess fat every 2 minutes until the skin is a crispy and golden brown. Turn the duck on to its flesh side and sear for 1 minute to lock in the juices. Transfer to an ovenproof dish, skin-side down again, and place in the preheated oven for 4 minutes. Remove and allow to rest for 4 minutes before serving.

Meanwhile, pan-fry the girolles and broad beans with a little butter for a few minutes until cooked.

Spread the chicken liver velouté neatly in the middle of the four serving plates. Cut each duck leg ballotine into two pieces and place one piece over the chicken liver on each plate. Slice and arrange the duck breast evenly between the four plates, add the Girolles and broad beans and finish with the jus. Enjoy!

Martha Kearney's BEEHIVE CAKE

Radio 4 presenter Martha Kearney is a part-time beekeeper and keen baker at her home in Suffolk. She created this impressive bake when she took part in Comic Relief Bake Off in 2013. Serves 14-16.

Ingredients

For the cake:

400g butter, softened

400g sugar

Grated zest of 2 lemons (you will use the juice for the buttercream)

2 tbsp honey

7 free-range eggs

400g self-raising flour, sifted

For the buttercream:

1kg butter, softened

1.5kg icing sugar, sifted, plus extra for dusting

Lemon juice

1 tbsp honey, or to taste

Golden-yellow colouring (rather than lemon)

For the decoration:

Small amounts of ready-to-roll fondant icing in yellow, black, red and white

25g flaked almonds

250g ready-to-roll green fondant icing

Method

Preheat the oven to 180°C. Grease and line a 6 inch round cake tin and a 7 inch round cake tin. Grease a 6 inch round ovenproof bowl. Cut out a small circle of baking paper to fit in the bottom of the bowl. Flour the sides.

Cream the butter and sugar until very pale, light and fluffy. Beat in the lemon zest and honey.

Add the eggs slowly, one at a time, plus a little of the flour if the batter looks like it may curdle. Fold in the remaining flour with a large metal spoon. Divide the mixture between the cake tins and the ovenproof bowl.

Bake in the preheated oven for 40-50 minutes, checking the smaller cakes after 30 minutes. The cakes are done when a skewer inserted into the centre of the cake comes out clean. Remove from the oven and cool in the tins for 10 minutes, before turning out onto a wire rack to cool completely. Remove the baking paper carefully.

For the buttercream, beat the softened butter in a free-standing mixer for 5-8 minutes until very light and soft. Add the icing sugar gradually, beating all the time, until it is all incorporated. Loosen the mixture with a little lemon juice and flavour with the honey, adding extra to taste if needed. Beat the golden-yellow food colouring into the buttercream to achieve your desired shade.

For the decoration, dust the work surface with icing sugar. Knead the yellow fondant icing until soft and pliable, then roll small amounts of the yellow fondant into rugby balls to form the body of the bees. Knead the black icing until soft and roll out on the dusted work surface into very thin ropes to create stripes. Brush the bees very lightly with water and stick on the stripes. Roll tiny balls of red for noses and little balls of white with black dots for eyes. Stick these on with a tiny dab of water. Push two flakes of almond into each bee for wings. Use some more black icing to create a door for the hive. Set aside to dry.

Roll out the white fondant icing and use a daisy cutter to cut out white daisies. Cut small circles from the yellow fondant for the centres of the daisies and stick on with a little water. Set aside to dry.

Place the largest cake on a cake board. Spread a layer of the buttercream on the top, then top with the smaller cake. Spread a little more buttercream on the top and then finish with the round bowl cake.

Spread a thin layer of buttercream all over the outside of the cake. Set aside to harden (preferably in the fridge) for 10-15 minutes.

Transfer the remaining buttercream to a piping bag fitted with a plain ¾ inch nozzle. Pipe the icing around the outside of the cake in concentric circles to create a hive shape. On the top, pipe a spiral and smooth with a palette knife.

Place a few bees on skewers or cocktail sticks and stick into the cake. Attach other bees directly to the hive, using a little water to stick them in place. Finish by sticking on the daisies.

Preserving TRADITIONS

From Granny's recipe to national retail, Mrs Bennett's Pickles & Chutneys are bringing traditional flavours to contemporary food-lovers.

Pickling is a family tradition in the Bennett household. Generations of the family have been preserving local fruits and vegetables in this age-old way, and now Keeley has taken on the mantle.

For Keeley, it all started with piccalilli. Its vibrant yellow colour, heady aroma and bold flavour are the same today as they were when Keeley's grandmother used to make it. Although back then, Keeley called it "pickled-willy", much to her gran's amusement!

Surprisingly, after decades of chutney-making, it was only a couple of years ago that Keeley decided to turn their family craft into a business. And it was all down to a Scotch egg.

Keeley's brother serves a wicked Scotch egg in his deli, Wrights of Frinton. And every good Scotch egg needs a good piccalilli to complement it, so she started making their family recipe for the deli. It went down a storm with customers and, inspired by its reception, Mrs Bennett's Pickles & Chutneys was born.

Today the range includes the traditional classics (the piccalilli is still made to her grandmother's secret recipe, which nobody outside the family knows!) and some modern combinations too – try the Plum and Port Chutney with slow-roast pork or give the Chilli Jam a go with some cream cheese.

One thing that has remained unchanged is the commitment to the finest quality ingredients. Using locally sourced produce and the finest ingredients available ensures every batch is at its absolute best. This is a family business that is passionate about the provenance of its ingredients and honouring its Suffolk heritage, and Mrs Bennett is proud to put her name on every jar.

With awards aplenty, new flavours in the pipeline and recognition coming from far and wide, it's all hands on deck in the Bennett family to keep up with ever-increasing demand. With the range now available in Marks & Spencer, this Suffolk success story is set to continue for generations to come.

MRS. BENNETT'S
PICKLES & CHUTNEYS
TOMATO AND GARLIC RELISH
MADE IN SUFFOLK
MRS. BENNETT'S
PICKLES & CHUTNEYS
CHILLI JAM
MADE IN SUFFOLK
MRS. BENNETT'S
PICKLES & CHUTNEYS
PLUM AND PORT CHUTNEY
MADE IN SUFFOLK
MRS. BENNETT'S
PICKLES & CHUTNEYS
APPLE AND GINGER CHUTNEY
MADE IN SUFFOLK
MRS. BENNETT'S
PICKLES & CHUTNEYS
PICCALILLI
MADE IN SUFFOLK
MRS. BENNETT'S
PICKLES & CHUTNEYS
PEAR AND WALNUT CHUTNEY
MADE IN SUFFOLK
MRS. BENNETT'S
PICKLES & CHUTNEYS
ONION MARMALADE
MADE IN SUFFOLK
MRS. BENNETT'S
PICKLES & CHUTNEYS
PEAR AND WALNUT CHUTNEY
MADE IN SUFFOLK
MRS. BENNETT'S
PICKLES & CHUTNEYS
PICCALILLI
MADE IN SUFFOLK
MRS. BENNETT'S
PICKLES & CHUTNEYS
CHILLI JAM
MADE IN SUFFOLK
MRS. BENNETT'S
PICKLES & CHUTNEYS
TOMATO AND GARLIC RELISH
MADE IN SUFFOLK
MRS. BENNETT'S
PICKLES & CHUTNEYS
APPLE AND GINGER CHUTNEY
MADE IN SUFFOLK
MRS. BENNETT'S
PICKLES & CHUTNEYS
PICCALILLI
MADE IN SUFFOLK
MRS. BENNETT'S
PICKLES & CHUTNEYS
PEAR AND WALNUT CHUTNEY
MADE IN SUFFOLK

Mrs Bennett's Pickles
BREAKFAST EGG

This is the perfect accompaniment to Mrs Bennett's Pickles & Chutneys Piccalilli. It's where the story began and it's still a firm favourite in the Bennett family. It's best to fill the sink with soapy water before you start making scotch eggs, so that you can wash your hands as you go. If you don't fancy the black pudding, simply make up the quantity with sausage meat instead. For an extra-tasty, rich egg, try using a duck egg, but increase the initial boiling time slightly. Makes 6.

Ingredients

7 large eggs

300g sausage meat

100g black pudding

2 tbsp fresh sage leaves, finely chopped

100g plain flour

200g white breadcrumbs (made from a slightly stale white loaf, crusts removed)

12 rashers of streaky bacon

800ml sunflower oil, for deep-frying

Salt and black pepper

Mrs Bennett's Pickles & Chutneys Piccalilli, to serve

Method

Preheat a deep-fryer to 150°C or place the sunflower oil in a large saucepan and heat it to 150°C using a cooking thermometer.

Place 6 of the eggs in a pan of cold water and bring to the boil. Boil for 5-6 minutes to obtain a soft yolk, then run under cold water to stop any further cooking. Peel and wash the eggs until they are completely shell-free.

Mix the sausage meat, black pudding, sage, some salt and pepper and a little water together with your hands until completely combined.

Fill one bowl with the flour (this is just for your hands) and another with the breadcrumbs. Beat the unused egg in another bowl.

With floured hands, mould each egg with the sausage mix until completely covered and then wrap each egg in 2 rashers of streaky bacon.

Dip and roll each egg in the beaten egg, then coat in the breadcrumbs until fully covered. Place on a plate close to your fryer or saucepan.

Once your oil has reached 150°C, carefully place the eggs into the fryer using a spoon. It is best to cook them in small batches – two at a time. Fry for 4-6 minutes or until a lovely golden colour. Remove the eggs from the fryer using a slotted spoon and place them on a plate lined with kitchen roll.

Repeat the process until all of the eggs are cooked.

Serve with salad and a large dollop of Mrs Bennett's Pickles & Chutneys Piccalilli.

Mindful MUNCHING

From simple snacks and breakfast sprinkles to salad toppers and sweet treats, Lucinda Clay aims to have us all tucking into nutritious nibbles.

Growing up in a quiet corner of New Zealand's south island, a healthy approach to life comes naturally to Lucinda. "My childhood was spent outdoors," she reminisces, "we burnt a lot of energy running around the Marlborough countryside, which in those days was inhabited mainly by sheep." To keep her hungry grandchildren's hands out of the sweet jar, her grandmother began toasting seeds, so that there was always a healthy snack to hand. Nutritious, delicious and packed full of energy, these became a firm favourite with her active family.

"We used to sit in the garden with a jar of toasted seeds, lick our fingers and dip them in," says Lucinda, and from these humble beginnings, her granny transformed this family recipe into a successful business.

Life took an unexpected turn when Lucinda met her boyfriend (now her husband), Suffolk-born Crispin, in Australia. Once they were happily settled in the unique Suffolk countryside among the golden fields of rapeseed, they were inspired to try to bring Lucinda's granny's success to the UK.

16 years ago this was no small feat. Seeds, now much celebrated in trendy healthy-eating circles, back then weren't a mainstay of the British diet. Not to mention the problem of where to acquire a roaster! When a friend who made coffee bean roasters in Africa heard, he offered to scale down his design and create them a unique roasting oven. And this ambitious husband and wife team have never looked back.

They have three bespoke roasters running daily, producing on average eight roasts a day, to keep up with demand for their unique seed mixes. Seeds are carefully sourced from around world, but the favourites are the local rape seeds from their neighbours and friends at Hill Farm Oil. Linseed and hemp seeds are also sourced locally where possible.

High in Omega 3, seeds pack a nutritional punch – with protein, fibre and minerals all wrapped up in these miniature superfood heroes. With eight mouthwatering flavours to choose from, Munchy Seeds have developed a pack to tempt every taste bud, spice up every salad and keep all of our fingers out of the biscuit tin.

With a string of accolades under their belts, booming online sales and unrivalled success at local food shows, this lovingly nurtured business is growing from strength to strength.

macpac

Munchy Seeds POWER SALAD

with Asian dressing

For a nutritious meal packed with protein, this salad is a winner. Not only does it contain all the flavour and health benefits of a Munchy Seeds mix, it contains a medley of wholesome vegetables, delicious salty feta and a tempting Asian dressing. For a vegetarian option, simply replace the chicken with tofu, or for fish-lovers, it's also nice with tinned tuna. Serves 4.

Ingredients

For the salad:

3 skinless chicken breasts

½ butternut squash, peeled, deseeded and cut into cubes

100g bag of spinach

100g bag of watercress

50g sundried tomatoes, chopped

3 small cooked beetroot, chopped

A handful of sprouted mung beans (optional, see instructions below for sprouting your own)

200g packet of feta

½ red onion, thinly sliced

¼ cucumber, chopped

1 tsp chopped fresh mint leaves

100g Munchy Seeds Pumpkin Power mix

Cold-pressed rapeseed oil, for drizzling

Butter, for greasing

Salt and pepper

For the Asian dressing:

90ml rice vinegar

160ml sunflower oil

80ml cold-pressed rapeseed oil

30ml soy sauce

½ tsp ground ginger

1 clove garlic, crushed

1 tsp sugar

Method

Preheat the oven to 200°C (180°C fan).

Place the skinless chicken breasts in a baking dish, drizzle with rapeseed oil and season with salt and pepper. Cover with buttered greaseproof paper (buttered-side down).

Place the butternut squash cubes on a baking tray, drizzle with rapeseed oil and season with salt and pepper.

Place the chicken and butternut squash in the preheated oven. Bake the chicken for about 30-40 minutes, until cooked through and the juices run clear. Bake the butternut squash for 35 minutes, until soft and beginning to brown at the edges. Set the chicken and squash aside to cool.

Place all the Asian dressing ingredients into an empty jam jar or vinaigrette dressing container, place the lid on tightly and shake vigorously until combined.

Combine the salad leaves, chicken, roasted squash, sundried tomatoes, beetroot, mung beans, cucumber, feta, red onion and fresh mint in a salad bowl. Dress with the Asian dressing and sprinkle over the Munchy Seeds Pumpkin Power mix last of all. (This way the lightly roasted pumpkin, sunflower and sesame seeds will stick to the salad leaves and not all disappear to the bottom of your salad.)

If you're taking this to work, pack the dressing and Munchy Seeds mix separately and add just before eating.

Sprouting your own mung beans

Freshly sprouted mung beans are delicious and have a nice nutty flavour. They are naturally high in essential minerals and vitamins, they are easily digested and they contain high amounts of fibre. Pour enough mung beans into an empty jam jar or see-through container to cover the bottom. Fill with luke warm tap water and leave over night to soak with the lid on, but not screwed on tightly. Next morning, tip the water out and flush with fresh water, then replace the lid. Leave the jar on the window sill (or by your Aga, if you have one) to grow. Flush with fresh water each morning and night. Allow a good 3-4 days for the mung beans to sprout. They will keep in the fridge for up to 2-3 days.

Festival Fever in BURY ST EDMUNDS

A picturesque market town in Suffolk, Bury St Edmunds brings the old and the new together with something for all the family. Ourburystedmunds celebrates everything that makes this quintessentially English town such a special place to live in, visit and explore.

From the ruins of the medieval abbey to the modern shops of the arc shopping centre, centuries of history have shaped the town into a thriving hub of independent shops, large stores, restaurants, cafés, bars and pubs. Renowned shopping takes place amongst the medieval grid and side streets, and Bury St Edmunds boasts the only Cathedral in Suffolk, as well as one of the few remaining Regency theatres in the country.

For many people here, there is a wonderful focus on food, which is reflected in the wide variety of independent and national restaurants, cafés and eateries (over 90 in fact) ranging from formal to informal and covering an awe-inspiring amount of diverse food cultures. If you'd rather get cooking at home, you'll find a large number of retailers selling local ingredients, fresh produce and home-made food products, as well as independent kitchen shops that sell absolutely everything you could need for the most sophisticated of kitchen, it is also one of a handful of destinations that still has a regular provisions market every Wednesday and Saturday, where you can rely on getting your hands on the freshest fruit, vegetables, meat, poultry, eggs and cheese from local farms, with plenty more to boot.

What is Ourburystedmunds? It is the local Business Improvement District (BID) for Bury St Edmunds. It is funded by businesses within the town centre, where the vast majority automatically become members of the Business Improvement District. The majority of activity that the town does for its businesses, its residents and its visitors simply wouldn't be possible without the BID. The whole ethos is to provide additional services and support to business members beyond what the public authorities are able to deliver. This commitment results in continual improvements in what the area has to offer, drawing people in to visit the vibrant town.

THE BODY SHOP
ELCOME TO BURY ST EDMUNDS
CLASS

Ourburystedmunds regularly organises events such as the Whitsun Fayre over the late May Bank Holiday and the Christmas Light Switch-On in November. One of the most popular events is the Food & Drink Festival that is held over the August Bank Holiday. In this foodie town, it is an event that draws in thousands of people, both regulars and visitors alike.

It features a demonstration kitchen with two celebrity chefs each year and a selection of chefs from some of the town's own eateries, who display their skills and recipes to the crowds across the two days. A large selection of food and drink stalls around the town centre are on hand to feed hungry guests, as well as a farmers market for buying ingredients to take home. The kids won't be left out either with a mini farm and a beach to explore. There's fun and food for all the family!

Later in the year, it's time for the Christmas Fayre – another fantastic annual event that is held over the last weekend in November. Such a hit in the past, it has now become an internationally recognised market with an impressive variety of stalls. From warming cups of mulled wine to classic Christmas pudding, the Christmas Fayre is somewhere to pick up everything you need for an enjoyable Christmas, support Suffolk producers and get in the festive spirit with the help of the local community.

If you'd like to find out more about these fabulous events and all the other things going on in Bury St Edmunds, visit www.ourburystedmunds.com

LORD'S AND THE FULNESS

In just a couple of years, Palfrey & Hall has gone from artisan start-up to one of the most celebrated new businesses in Suffolk. It's all for the love of meat.

You could certainly say that this meat-obsessed pair are a cut above the rest when it comes to butchery. Offering an unrivalled bespoke cutting, curing and smoking service, Shaun Palfrey and Deaglan Hall sure know their shoulder from their shank.

Racking up an impressive 25 years' butchery experience between them, Shaun and Deaglan decided they wanted to do something a little bit different and bring together their butchery skills and passion for flavour in an ambitious business partnership.

When their friends at Kenton Hall Estate mentioned they were considering building a cutting room on site to butcher their Longhorn cattle (an ancient native English breed), the pair jumped at the chance to set up their own business there. Two years down the line and it's flourished.

Locally-reared meat arrives here directly from the abattoir, travelling just a few miles down Suffolk country roads – no air miles here! They know the provenance of each and every animal, from the cattle, pigs and lambs to goats and even water buffalo, which are farmed just a few miles down the road.

The butchery service is the cornerstone of the business. The innovative pair don't shy away from breaking convention and will happily go for adventurous and unusual cuts. Simply choose how you want your animal cut and for how long you want it to hang, and your wish is their command.

Pop along and ask about their bacon. Real bacon. Cut, cured and smoked on site. No water is pumped into your rashers, so it's a world away from anything you can buy in the supermarket. In fact both their smoked back and streaky bacon were awarded two gold stars at the Great Taste Awards, and their cooked smoked ham boasts the same claim to fame.

The Suffolk black bacon is cured using ale from the brewery at Earl Soham, which they mix with dark, sticky molasses and black treacle for a distinctly deep, rich taste. It's available at local retailers, but you can always drop by, say hello and buy some direct too.

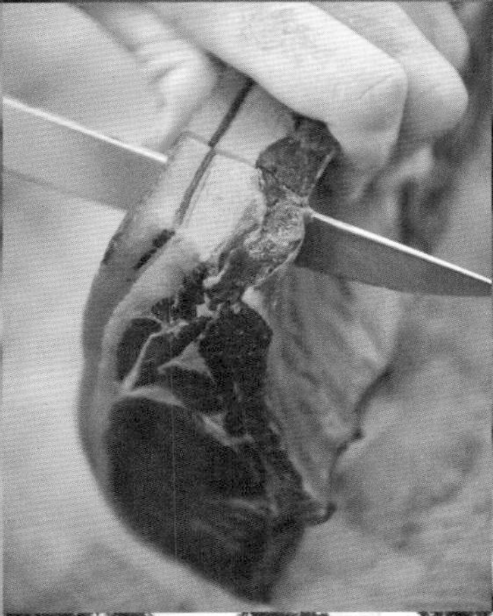

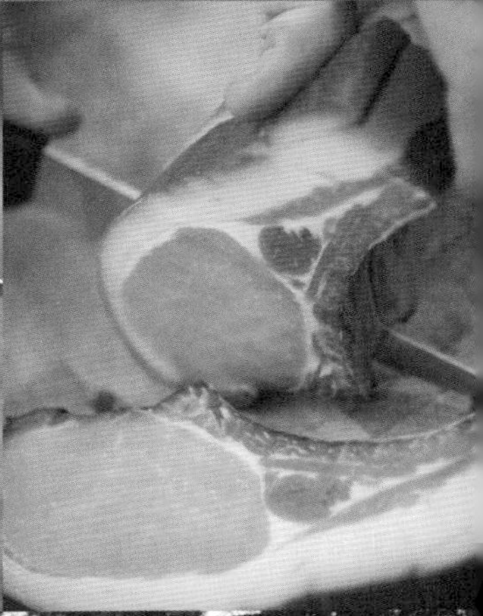

Palfrey & Hall
SUFFOLK BLACK BACON CHOP

with braised red cabbage, mash and Aspall cider sauce

Famous for their incredible smoking flavours, Palfrey and Hall serve up one of their favourite ways to enjoy their delicious Suffolk black bacon. This hearty supper celebrates all things Suffolk on one plate – tuck in! Serves 4.

Ingredients

For the red cabbage:

40g unsalted butter

½ red cabbage, shredded

1 Granny Smith apple, peeled, cored and cut into chunks

2 tbsp light brown muscavado sugar

½ tsp ground cinnamon

½ tsp ground mixed spice

125ml cider vinegar

100ml water

For the mashed potatoes:

900g floury potatoes, such as Maris Piper or King Edwards, peeled and cut into large chunks

2 tbsp butter

A pinch of sea salt and cracked black pepper

A splash of double cream (or milk)

For the Aspall Cider sauce:

1 tbsp butter

2 white onions, sliced

1 tsp sugar

100ml Aspall cider (Harry Sparrow)

2 tbsp wholegrain mustard

100ml double cream

A pinch of sea salt and cracked black pepper

For the bacon chop:

4 x Palfrey & Hall Suffolk beer and treacle bacon chops or steaks (or smoked bacon)

Method

For the red cabbage, put half the butter in a large saucepan and melt slowly over a medium heat. Add the shredded red cabbage, apple chunks, sugar and spices. Mix well and braise for about 10 minutes, stirring constantly to prevent burning.

After add the cider vinegar and water. Simmer for 50 minutes over a low to medium heat, stirring occasionally.

Meanwhile, turn your attention to the chops, mashed potatoes and sauce, so that you can have everything ready to serve at the same time. Preheat the oven to 200°C (fan 180°C).

Heat a frying pan over a medium heat and sear the bacon chop on both sides until browned. Transfer to the preheated oven and cook for about 15 minutes until cooked through.

For the mashed potatoes, boil the potatoes in a large pan of lightly salted water for about 20 minutes until tender. Drain, add the butter, seasoning and cream, and mash until smooth. Set aside and keep warm.

For the sauce, heat the butter in a saucepan over a medium heat, add the sliced onions and fry until softened. Add the sugar and cook, stirring, until the onions brown. Add the cider and mustard and bring to a simmer. Finally add the cream and cook for about 5 minutes until thick. Season to taste.

Finish off the red cabbage by adding the remaining butter, then stir to give it a glossy shine. Serve the chop with the mashed potatoes, cider sauce and braised cabbage.

Local deli and bustling café by day, bistro-style restaurant with wine and cocktails by night... The Pantry in Newmarket has got it all covered.

There is much more to this pantry than the name lets on. Of course you can grab your store-cupboard basics here, but Vincent and Anne-Marie, husband and wife owners, have brought together in one place a whole host of incredible offerings from all over East Anglia. If there is something delicious being produced in Suffolk, you'll most likely be able to find it in their welcoming deli.

Norfolk and Suffolk cheeses are on offer, including Suffolk Gold from the wonderful Suffolk Farmhouse Cheeses, as well as hams, bacon, salami and chorizo from Lane Farm in Brundish – locally reared pigs, locally cured and utterly delicious. It's possible to spend hours perusing the olives and antipasti, chutneys and jams, loose-leaf teas and fine coffees, and of course the freshly made cakes and artisan breads, too.

It's the personal touch that sets Vincent and Anne-Marie apart from other stores. If you're looking for something a bit different, just ask – they'll do their best to source ingredients from their suppliers, help with dinner party catering and even prepare business lunches.

During the day time there are freshly made sandwiches, quiches, sausage rolls and cakes aplenty, but in the evening, The Pantry transforms into a bistro-style restaurant with an open kitchen where diners can enjoy watching Vincent and his team put together traditional British classics, showcasing the best of the regional produce.

Working closely (literally!) with their neighbours, fresh meat comes from Eric Tennant's butchers and the fish comes from Fish! of Burwell. Some of the dishes have proved so popular, such as the rib eye steak and Vince's triple chocolate brownies, they wouldn't dare remove them from the menu, but the specials board is always changing with seasonal offerings and inspired ideas to tempt the taste buds.

The evening menu is accompanied by wines and cocktails, and the atmosphere is laid-back yet stylish, perfectly suited to the bistro-style food being enjoyed. This is the perfect place to spend an evening with friends – sit back, relax and enjoy the charming ambience and thoroughly fantastic food.

THE PANTRY
THE PANTRY
THE PANTRY
The CAMBRIDGESHIRE Cook Book £14.95
THE CAMBRIDGESHIRE
THE PANTRY
FINE FOOD SHOP AND EATERY
THE PANTRY
FINE FOOD SHOP & EATERY
THE PANTRY
FINE FOOD SHOP & EATERY
THE PANTRY
ROASTED RED PEPPERS
The Fine Cheese co
Pickled Figs
£6.50

The Pantry
BLYTHBURGH PORK CHOP

with home-made black pudding and butterbean stew

The taste of home-made black pudding is worth the effort of sourcing the ingredients, and it works exceptionally well with good-quality free-range pork chops. You will need to soak the butter beans overnight. Serves 4.

Ingredients

400ml ham stock (or chicken stock)

500g butter beans, soaked overnight and drained

4 Blythburgh pork chops, French-trimmed

200g black pudding, cut into cubes (see below for home-made black pudding)

100ml white wine

15g chopped parsley

Grated zest of 1 lemon

For the black pudding:

1kg back fat

1kg dried pigs' blood

300g dried oats

2 litres water

20g mixed spice

20g pepper

20g salt

Method

Start by making the black pudding. Chop the back fat into chunks and mix with all the other black pudding ingredients. Refrigerate for 30 minutes, then roll the mixture into cylinders and wrap in cling film. Cook in a water bath for 1 hour at 150°C until the black pudding reaches 77°C.

Bring the ham stock (or chicken stock) to the boil in a saucepan, add the soaked butter beans and cook for about 1 hour until soft. Drain the beans, reserving the stock. Set both the beans and stock aside.

Cook the pork chops in a frying pan, starting on the skin side - use a small tin to prop them up in the pan if needed. Once cooked through, set aside to rest and keep warm. Fry the black pudding cubes until crispy on all sides.

Add the wine to a large pan over high heat and reduce by half, then add the beans, black pudding, parsley, lemon zest and enough stock to cover. Warm through, then serve with the pork chops in warmed bowls.

Smooth SAILING

With twins Alex and Oliver Burnside at the helm, The Plough & Sail has become one of the Suffolk coast's premier destinations for relaxed dining.

There's no separating twin brothers Alex and Oliver Burnside from the beautiful Suffolk coastal region where they have always lived and worked. Gazing over the picturesque setting on the River Alde, in the wonderful Snape Maltings, it's clear why they chose the Plough & Sail as the ideal place to start their family business.

Having both worked in the food industry for 10 years, they built up experience in renowned local restaurants in their respective fields – front of house management for Alex and working his way up through the kitchens for Oliver – before making the decision to start their own business.

Their aim was to create a welcoming place where people can enjoy good-quality seasonal food and choose from a varied selection of drinks in a relaxed environment.

Heading up front of house, Alex ensures every customer is well looked after. He's happy to discuss the extensive wine list and carefully considered draught lagers and ales, helping diners to match their drinks to their food choices.

The specials board changes regularly, depending on seasonal availability, but the menu is based on classic British dishes, peppered with modern twists, inspiration from around the world and plenty of creative flair.

Oliver likes to focus on simple food cooked to perfection. His Dover sole is his brother's favourite dish and naturally a consistent winner on the menu. The scallops are crowd-pleasers too and they appear regularly on the specials board due to popular demand.

The high ceilings give the restaurant a light and airy feel, but the older original section of the pub has cosy corners that are perfect for enjoying a quiet drink. With the intimate balcony area and attractive courtyard too, the Plough & Sail ticks all the boxes for year-round dining.

ADNAMS
SOUTHWOLD
WOODFORDE'S
NELSON'S
The Plough & Sail
THE
PLOUGH
& SAIL
COUNTRY DINING PUB
FREEHOUSE
enjoy
lunch in
our
Sunny
Courtyard
PLOUGH & SAIL
COUNTRY DINING PUB
FREEHOUSE

The Plough & Sail

PAN-FRIED SCOTTISH SCALLOPS

with herb mash, chorizo jam, wilted spinach and pea purée

This recipe was jointly created by co-owner and head chef Oliver Burnside and sous chef Chris Selby. This flavour combination never fails to please, and it would make an excellent dish to impress with at a dinner party. The chorizo jam can be made up to 24 hours in advance and stored in the fridge overnight. Serves 4.

Ingredients

For the chorizo jam:

1 large onion, sliced

10 rashers streaky bacon, sliced

400g chorizo, sliced

4 garlic cloves, finely chopped

140ml strong coffee (espresso if possible)

140ml cola

A dash of sherry vinegar

2 tbsp sugar

Rapeseed oil, for cooking

For the pea purée:

1 shallot, finely diced

140ml vegetable stock

200g frozen peas

Rapeseed oil, for cooking

For the herb mash:

4 large Maris Piper potatoes, peeled and cut into large chunks

140ml milk

140ml double cream

A large knob of butter

A bunch of parsley, chopped

Grated zest of 1 lemon (keep the juice for the scallops)

Salt and black pepper

For the scallops and wilted spinach:

16 large scallops (ask your fishmonger to prepare them ready for cooking)

A large knob of butter

1kg baby spinach, washed

Rapeseed oil, for cooking

Method

Start by making the chorizo jam. You can make it the day before and store it in the fridge overnight. Heat a little rapeseed oil in a pan set over a medium heat, add the sliced onion, bacon and chorizo and sweat them, stirring regularly, until browned. Drain away the excess fat, then add all the other ingredients and simmer for 30 minutes. Allow to cool slightly, then blitz in a food processor or blender to a coarse purée. Cover and chill until needed, but allow it to come to room temperature before serving.

For the pea purée, heat a little rapeseed oil in a pan over medium heat, add the diced shallot and sweat it, stirring regularly, until cooked. Add the stock, bring to the boil, then add the frozen peas. Bring back to the boil and simmer until tender, then blitz in a food processor or blender. Pass through a fine sieve to remove any lumps. Cover and set aside.

For the herb mash, boil the potatoes in a large pan of lightly salted water for about 10 minutes until tender, then drain. Bring the milk, cream and butter to the boil in a separate pan, then add the drained potatoes. Whisk or mash the mixture until smooth. Add the chopped parsley and lemon zest and mix well. Season with salt and pepper and set aside and keep warm.

To serve, warm the pea purée in a pan. Heat a large frying pan with a little rapeseed oil until smoking. Add the scallops and cook for 2 minutes on each side until golden brown. Towards the end of cooking, add the butter and squeeze in the reserved lemon juice. When the butter has melted, remove the scallops, keeping the cooking liquid. Add the spinach to pan and cook until wilted. Remove the spinach, draining the excess liquid. Serve the scallops and spinach with the herb mash and chorizo jam.

A Taste of VIETNAM

Close your eyes and transport yourself to Thao's mother's kitchen in Vietnam...

The inspirational story behind this enticing range of products begins far away from Suffolk, in a small kitchen in the historic Phuoc Long province of Vietnam. Thao spent her childhood chasing dragonflies, hunting for eggs and tucking into exotic fruits around her family home at the bottom of a mountain. She can still remember the fragrant aromas that wafted from her mother's small restaurant, where tourists came to escape the hustle and bustle of Saigon.

When the war arrived on their doorstep in 1975, Thao's life changed forever. Her father, who had been a translator for America's Special Forces (the Green Berets), was captured by the North Vietnamese army and sent away to one of the 're-education' camps. By 1984, life under the new regime had become unbearable for Thao and, at only 12 years old, she left her family and all she knew behind and escaped on a small fishing boat with 70 other refugees.

After 10 days drifting at sea with a broken propeller, the boat was rescued and taken to Indonesia. After spending 7 months in a children's home, Thao was resettled in Denmark, where she was eventually reunited with her family. Today, she lives in Suffolk with her husband and daughter.

Thao launched Red Chilli Kitchen in 2014, so that others could taste the dishes she remembers from her mother's kitchen. Vietnamese food is light, fresh and fragrant, so it's no surprise the distinctive flavours of this healthy and colourful cuisine are now incredibly popular in the UK.

There are four products in the Red Chilli Kitchen range: a deliciously aromatic curry paste, a luscious tomato chilli jam blended with lemongrass, a spicy tomato marinade and a piquant dressing blended with ginger, garlic, chilli and lemon juice. Authentic, versatile and easy to use, Thao's tempting blends are spicing up stir-fries, salads, stews and curries across Suffolk. As they say in Vietnam: "Ăn Ngon" – eat well!

RED CHILLI KITCHEN
Vietnamese Curry Paste
RED CHILLI KITCHEN
Vietnamese Tomato Chilli Jam
RED CHILLI KITCHEN
Vietnamese Miracle Dressing and Marinade
RED CHILLI KITCHEN
Vietnamese Tomato Marinade

Red Chilli Kitchen

PRAWN, PORK & CUCUMBER SALAD

Gỏi Dưa Leo Tôm Thịt

Thao's Miracle Dressing and Marinade is an authentic blend of ginger, garlic, chilli, lemon juice and fish sauce. In Vietnam this recipe is famously known as *Nước Chấm* and it can be found on every dining table across the country, with many variations of the recipe. The delicate balance of sweet, salty and sour makes it an irresistible concoction and it is delicious as a dipping sauce, salad dressing or marinade. It is fantastic on this vibrant salad, which is fresh, light and full of the flavours of Vietnam. Serves 4.

Ingredients

500g raw, unpeeled king pawns, heads removed

2 tbsp Red Chilli Kitchen Miracle Dressing and Marinade, plus extra for drizzling

200g pork shoulder

1 tsp sea salt

1 onion, peeled and halved

2 cucumbers, halved lengthways

1 large carrot, peeled and sliced into julienne

2 small red onions, peeled and thinly sliced

1½ tbsp sugar

2 tbsp roasted peanuts, crushed

Fresh mint or coriander leaves for garnish

Method

Rinse the prawns. Slice the prawns with a sharp knife along the length of their back (do not cut all the way through) and remove the black vein.

Marinate the prawns with the Red Chilli Kitchen Miracle Dressing and Marinade for 1 hour in the fridge. Meanwhile, preheat the oven to 225°C (fan 205°C).

Cover a baking tray with baking paper and arrange the prawns in a single layer on the tray. Cook the prawns in the preheated oven for 10-12 minutes or until the shells are pink. Allow to cool, then peel.

Place the pork in a pot with the salt and halved onion. Fill the pot with cold water (so the top of water is about 5cm above the pork). Bring to the boil, then turn the heat down to low, cover with a lid and simmer for 30 minutes, or until the pork is cooked through. Remove the pork from the pot and set aside to cool. Once the pork has cooled, slice it thinly.

Remove the seeds from the cucumber halves with a spoon and then slice the cucumber thinly. Place the cucumber slices in a colander with the sliced carrot and red onions, and sprinkle over the sugar. Leave for 20 minutes for the sugar to draw the liquid from the vegetables. After this time, squeeze the remaining liquid out of the vegetables.

Place the vegetables, prawns and pork into a salad bowl. Just before serving, drizzle some Red Chilli Kitchen Miracle Dressing and Marinade over the salad and toss well. Garnish with the crushed peanuts and fresh mint or coriander.

Red Chilli Kitchen

BEEF STEW

Bò Kho

This is one of Vietnam's most popular dishes. Whilst no one can agree from which part of Vietnam this dish originates, it was the French who (during their colonial occupation of Indochina) introduced beef to Vietnam. The slow-cooked beef, carrots and blend of lemongrass, star anise and paprika make this a succulent, sweet and fragrant dish. Due to the French influence on Vietnamese cuisine, many will serve this stew with a fresh baguette instead of rice. The Red Chilli Kitchen Tomato Marinade is also suitable for vegetarians – simply replace the beef with tofu. Serves 4.

Ingredients

1kg beef brisket, cut into 3-4cm pieces

4 heaped tbsp Red Chilli Kitchen Tomato Marinade

1 tbsp rapeseed oil

1 large onion, peeled and cut into thick wedges

1 litre unsweetened coconut water (not coconut milk!)

3 large carrots, peeled and cut into large chunks

Sea salt

Method

Place the beef and Red Chilli Kitchen Tomato Marinade into a mixing bowl. Mix well, rubbing the marinade into the beef. Cover the bowl and marinate for 2 hours in the fridge or, for best results, overnight. Take the beef out of the fridge 30 minutes before cooking.

Heat the oil in a thick-bottomed flameproof casserole. Remove some of the excess marinade from the beef and set it aside to add later. Brown the beef all over in the hot oil, then stir in the onion wedges and the remaining marinade from the mixing bowl. Add the coconut water and bring to the boil. Put the lid on the casserole, reduce to a slow simmer and cook gently for about 3½ hours, stirring occasionally.

45 minutes before the end, add the carrots and cook until the meat and carrots are tender. Season with salt. Serve with a green salad and either rice or a fresh baguette.

Red Chilli Kitchen

CHICKEN & SWEET POTATO CURRY

Cà Ri Gà

This Vietnamese curry is deliciously different from other Asian curries! The blend of chilli, ginger, garlic and lemongrass makes this an alluring dish. Each region has its own variation of this recipe. In central Vietnam they prefer to use more chilli, whereas in South Vietnam they add coconut milk. Thao has taken the ingredients from this wonderful dish and distilled them down into a beautifully balanced aromatic paste. This dish is suitable for vegetarians – simply use tofu instead of chicken. Serves 4.

Ingredients

1kg chicken thighs

4 tbsp Red Chilli Kitchen Curry Paste

4 tbsp rapeseed oil

3 large sweet potatoes, peeled and cut into 2.5cm cubes

2 shallots, peeled and cut into small wedges

3 large carrots, peeled and cut into 4cm pieces

200ml coconut milk

500ml water

Sea salt

Method

Place the chicken thighs and curry paste into a bowl. Ensure the paste is rubbed well into the chicken. Cover the bowl and marinate for 2 hours in the fridge or, for best results, overnight. Take the chicken out of the fridge 30 minutes before cooking.

Heat the oil in a large wok over a medium heat. Add the sweet potatoes and fry for about 5-8 minutes until golden. Use a slotted spoon to transfer the sweet potatoes on to a sheet of kitchen roll. Discard some of the excess oil from the wok.

Remove the excess curry paste from the chicken and set aside to add later. Add the chicken to the wok and cook over a medium heat until lightly golden all over. Add the shallots and carrots and fry for a few minutes, then add the remaining curry paste, coconut milk and water and bring to the boil. Reduce to a simmer, cover the wok and cook for 30 minutes.

Add the sweet potatoes and simmer for 10 minutes more, or until the chicken and potatoes are tender. Season with salt. Serve with rice or simply with a fresh baguette and salad.

For the perfect basmati rice

Rinse the rice in a saucepan of cold water, stirring it several times in order to remove the starch. Drain the water and repeat the process 2-3 times. Pour boiling water over the rice to cover by no more than 2cm. Bring the water back to a boil, stir and then turn down the heat to a very low simmer. Cover with a lid and leave for 20 minutes. Don't remove the lid during this time. When the rice is perfectly cooked, there will be no water remaining in the saucepan.

Locally SAUCED

Salubrious Sauce Company, a welcome newcomer to the British condiment market, is breathing new life into breakfasts across Suffolk and beyond.

It all started with a lively debate across the breakfast table one morning. James Fennell was preparing a fry-up with family and friends, and the all-too-familiar debate was occurring around him: Which was the king of the breakfast condiments, brown sauce or tomato sauce? For James, it was often a struggle to find enthusiasm for either camp.

He longed for something a little more "off-piste" to liven up his breakfast, and as a man who confesses to loving a challenge, he set himself the task of creating something himself. "I had in mind to create a breakfast sauce with more punch, zip and zing," says James.

Leaving his corporate career behind him, he embarked on a mission of batch after batch of recipe development, market research and branding. Along the way, he has taste-tested his product on the breakfast butties of committed ketchup fans and staunch brown sauce lovers.

He has learnt that people have very strong opinions about their morning condiments, that nothing polarises people quite like the red or brown debate, but that many people, like him, were also keen to try something new and exciting on their fry-up. He also discovered that he is a perfectionist through and through! Eventually, after months of hard work, British Breakfast Sauce was born.

British Breakfast Sauce is a unique product with a complex medley of flavourings: "It's fruity, smoky, woody, spicy and tangy." It's a classic British idea with a thoroughly modern edge. Look out for its distinctive bottles featuring Monty the British Bulldog as it appears on breakfast tables across Suffolk.

The future looks bright for this new kid on the block. With stockists snapping up the sauce and a new product in the pipeline, the British condiment aisle looks set for a shake-up.

Salubrious Sauce Co.

Salubrious Sauce Co.

FULL MONTY STRUDEL

and black pudding bombs

A fabulous British Breakfast Sauce needs a fabulous British breakfast to go with it. Here are two classics, reworked into irresistible contemporary creations. The full monty breakfast wrapped in filo pastry is ideal to pick up and dip into your sauce. And the best thing – it can be made the day before, so it just needs to be heated up in the morning. Serves 4-6.

Ingredients

For the strudel:

6 pork chipolatas

6 rashers smoked streaky bacon

150g mushrooms, sliced

1 small shallot, chopped

2 tbsp crème fraîche

1 tbsp mild mustard

100g strong cheddar, grated

250g tin of baked beans

4 hard-boiled eggs, peeled and roughly sliced

1 tsp chopped parsley

3 sheets filo pastry

Clarified butter, for brushing

A light oil, for frying

Salt and black pepper

For the black pudding bombs:

45g bag pork scratchings

50g black pudding

2 egg yolks

20g breadcrumbs

Oil, for deep-frying

Method

For the strudel:

In a frying pan, fry the chipolatas, bacon, mushrooms and shallot until golden and cooked through, drain on kitchen roll and allow to cool.

In a large mixing bowl, mix together the crème fraîche, mustard, baked beans and grated cheddar. Now add the cooled cooked ingredients along with the sliced eggs and chopped parsley. Season with a good pinch of salt and pepper and give it a final gentle mix.

Lay out the three sheets of filo and brush one side of each sheet with clarified butter. Layer the three sheets on top of each other. Now evenly place the mixture (you will need about 450g) in a line along the length of the pastry.

Roll the pastry tightly, keeping the sides flat to make a square log. For best results wrap in cling film and allow to set in the fridge for 1 hour (or up to 2 days).

When ready to cook, preheat the oven to 200°C (fan 180°C).

Remove the cling film. Heat a little light oil in an ovenproof frying pan and fry the strudel until all sides are golden brown. Transfer the pan to the preheated oven and finish cooking for 15 minutes. Remove and allow to rest for 5 minutes. To serve, slices it into shards with a sharp serrated knife and arrange on a warm plate.

For the black pudding bombs:

Heat the oil for deep-frying in a deep-fryer or a heavy-bottomed pan over a medium heat.

Place the pork scratchings in a food processor and whizz to a dust. Set aside.

Whizz the black pudding in the food processor, then mould it into balls the size of conkers.

Mix the breadcrumbs and pork scratching dust together.

Put the egg yolk in one bowl and the breadcrumb mix in another bowl. Roll the bombs first in the egg yolk, then in the breadcrumbs. Repeat to make sure they are fully coated.

Fry the balls in the hot oil until golden and crispy. Drain on kitchen roll and serve.

Scarlett & Mustard launched as a business by accident after the co-founder's son Ollie, aged 11, set up a stall outside the family home to sell his great grandmother's tarragon dressing – selling out after just 2 hours!

A little detective work is needed to uncover the identities behind the eye-catching Scarlett & Mustard branding. Sandy Ruddock (aka Miss Scarlett) and her husband Julian Pollard (Colonel Mustard) took their personas from the classic board game Cluedo.

The husband and wife team officially established the business in 2012 and, after a whirlwind few years, they now have 24 products in their impressive portfolio, including dressings, marinades, infused English rapeseed oils, savoury jams, relishes and a set of gloriously unusual fruit curds (think Rhubarb & Vanilla Curd or Toffee Apple Curd!).

One look at the intriguing labels with their upside-down fonts, bold colours and quirky designs, and it's obvious it's a family affair. From Miss Scarlett's Ornamental Ginger & Soy Sauce and The Colonel's Poppy Seed Dressing to Granny's Original Tarragon Dressing and Rudolph's Leftovers Curry Sauce, there is input from all the family team.

They have stacked up fifteen Great Taste Awards so far, and the products are stocked in some of the country's most prestigious food halls, including Harrods, Selfridges, Harvey Nichols and Booths, as well as over 750 independent farm shops, delis and food retailers.

"We want to make life as easy and tasty as possible for busy families – anyone can use our products either straight from the bottle or jar, or to cook with – they are incredibly versatile, user friendly and above all healthy. We use rapeseed oil from a local farm – this means not only are we supporting our local farmers, but rapeseed oil is fantastic to cook with as it has a high burn point, low saturated fat and greater levels of Omega 3,6 and 9 oils than olive oil, making it a great healthy alternative."

The ethos of the business is simple: to use, where possible, locally sourced ingredients, and to avoid using any artificial flavours, colours or additives. Customers can rely on the products to whip up quick and easy meals with no fuss – Just Add Food!

great
PRODUCER

ROSIE'S DOO DAH SAUCE
AUNTIE FROG'S LIME & CHILLI DRES SING
BIG BEAR'S HONEY DRES SING
SCARLETT'S ORNA MENTAL GINGER & SOY SAUCE

MUSTARD
TURNING FOOD ON ITS HEAD
THE DRESSING ROOM

BLACKCURRANT & STAR ANISE CURD
SCARLETT & MUSTARD
TURNING FOOD ON ITS HEAD
PASSIONFRUIT & LEMON CURD
LIME & MINT CURD
SCARLETT & MUSTARD
TURNING FOOD ON ITS HEAD

ORNA MENTAL GINGER & SOY SAUCE

SCARLETT & MUSTARD

PASSIONFRUIT & LEMON CURD
RHUBARB & VANILLA CURD
SCARLETT & MUSTARD
TOFFEE APPLE CURD
PASSIONFRUIT & LEMON CURD
RHUBARB & VANILLA CURD

Scarlett & Mustard
FRITTATA STARTER

Named after Sandy's stepson William who can consume a kilo of it in a week, Billy's Champion Chilli Jam is sweet, hot and tangy all at the same time. It acquired 'champion' in its name when it won a Great Taste Award before even hitting the shelves. It's just the thing to liven up eggs in this delicious frittata recipe. Serves 4.

Ingredients

6 eggs

1 jar of Billy's Champion Chilli Jam from Scarlett & Mustard

1 tbsp rapeseed oil

3-4 spring onions, peeled and chopped

75g feta cheese, crumbled

1 tbsp chopped fresh coriander, plus some extra sprigs to garnish

Salt and black pepper

Method

Whisk the eggs with a little salt and pepper, then beat in half the jar of Billy's Champion Chilli Jam.

Heat the rapeseed oil in a small non-stick frying pan over a low heat. Add the chopped spring onions and spread out, then pour in the egg mixture and leave to cook gently for about 5-7 minutes, or until the edges start to set.

Meanwhile, preheat the grill to high.

Once the edges have started to set, sprinkle over the crumbled feta cheese and chopped coriander, then put the frying pan under the hot grill for 2-3 minutes.

Turn out onto a platter and then serve with an extra dollop of Scarlett & Mustard Billy's Chilli Jam, sprigs of fresh coriander and some warm crusty bread. Mmmmm...!

SCARLETT'S
ORNA
MENTAL
INGER
SOY
SAUCE
SCARLETT'S
ORNA
MENTAL
INGER
SOY
SAUCE

Scarlett & Mustard

SCARLETT'S ORNAMENTAL

ginger & soy stir fry

This rich Oriental dressing was mistakenly called 'ornamental' by Sandy's daughter Chloe and the name stuck! This delicious product was the first Great Taste Award winner for Scarlett & Mustard. You can make this with beef, chicken or pork too – just thinly slice it and add it with the onions at the start. Serves 4.

Ingredients

1 small red onion, sliced

3 spring onions, sliced at an angle

1 clove garlic, crushed

1 red chilli, thinly sliced

2 tbsp rapeseed oil

A handful of mangetout, each sliced into 3 pieces

A handful of mushrooms, thickly sliced

A handful of green cabbage, sliced

A few water chestnuts, halved

1 bottle of Scarlett's Ornamental Ginger & Soy Sauce from Scarlett & Mustard

200g fresh rice or egg noodles

1 tbsp sesame seeds

A handful of fresh coriander leaves, roughly chopped

Method

Mix the red onion, spring onion, garlic and chilli together.

Heat a wok or large frying pan over a high heat and add the oil. When smoking, add the onion mixture and cook for a minute or two before adding the rest of the vegetables. Cook, stirring constantly, for 1-2 minutes. Add in the noodles and cook for a further 3-4 minutes, tossing and stirring frequently.

Finally, add 2-3 tablespoons of Scarlett's Ornamental Ginger & Soy Sauce, sprinkle over the sesame seeds and cook for a further few seconds.

Spoon into bowls. Drizzle over a little more Scarlett's Ornamental Ginger & Soy Sauce, and chopped fresh coriander and serve. Mmmmmmm…!

LIME
MINT
CURD
The Curd Herd
PASSIONFRUIT
& LEMON
CURD
great taste
SCARLETT
& MUSTARD

Scarlett & Mustard

A TRIO OF CURD PUDS

You can use any of our curds in any of the below recipes – mix and match as you please!

Ingredients

For the Blackcurrant & Star Anise Curd Biscuit Cake

250g unsalted butter

300g white chocolate, broken into bits

300g hobnobs or shortbread biscuits, broken into bits

1 jar of Blackcurrant & Star Anise Curd from Scarlett & Mustard

50g nuts (optional, macadamia or pecan both work well)

Icing sugar, for dusting

For the Passionfruit Curd Fool

1 jar of Passionfruit & Lemon Curd from Scarlett & Mustard

500g natural yoghurt

1 fresh passionfruit

Fresh mint leaves, to decorate

A handful of fresh berries to decorate, such as redcurrants or blueberries

For the Lime & Mint Curd Frozen Yoghurt

1 jar of Lime & Mint Curd from Scarlett & Mustard

500g natural yoghurt

Method

Blackcurrant & Star Anise Curd Biscuit Cake (Serves 6-8)

Melt the butter in a large pan and add in the white chocolate. Do not over work as it may separate.

Add the broken biscuits and stir in the Blackcurrant & Star Anise Curd. If you are using nuts, stir them in at this point.

Spoon into a small baking tray lined with greaseproof paper. Ease into the corners and compress lightly with a potato masher.

Refrigerate for several hours until set. Turn out onto a board and dust with icing sugar. Cut into squares and serve. This will keep in the fridge in an airtight container for 2-3 weeks. It also freezes well.

Passionfruit Curd Fool (Serves 4-6)

Simply mix the whole jar of Passionfruit & Lemon Curd into the yoghurt and spoon into small dessert dishes. Scoop out the insides of the passionfruit and drizzle a little on each portion. Decorate with fresh mint leaves and some fresh berries.

Lime & Mint Curd Frozen Yoghurt (Serves 4-6)

Mix half the jar of Lime & Mint Curd into the yoghurt and place in a Tupperware box. Place in the freezer for an hour or so. Take out and mix well, and return to the freezer for another hour. Take out again, spoon the rest of the jar of curd into the mix, and gently swirl in. Place back in the freezer for another 3-4 hours or until frozen. Serve with meringues or fresh fruit.

Culinary CLASSICS

Nick and Diane Barrett have created something special within the 16th century walls at Scutchers restaurant, and it has been drawing in the locals for over 20 years.

Accomplished cooking is the order of the day at Scutchers. With 38 years of experience behind him, Nick Barrett has been cooking since he left the classroom aged 16. The years of traditional training are evident in the ethos of the kitchen. This is proper cooking, and it's a joy to behold.

Nick and his wife Diane bought the attractive hall house, which dates back to 1530, 24 years ago. With Nick heading up the kitchen, Diane expertly taking charge of front of house and a long-standing set of loyal staff, this dedicated team have been rewarded with success after success… in fact their collection includes Good Food Guide awards and a Michelin Bib Gourmand.

However, this husband and wife duo don't have time to sit back and admire their accolades. When they are not running the restaurant, they are busy smoking their own salmon on the premises, which they supply all over the country – and feature on the restaurant menu of course.

It's this commitment to raw ingredients that sets this family-run business apart. The philosophy here is simple: proper food cooked well.

Fish and cuts of meat are all delivered whole to the restaurant, where they are filleted or butchered on site. Only by understanding the basics can chefs really do ingredients justice, and, as they source the finest possible ingredients from around the UK, doing them justice is a priority here.

Loyal customers return time and time again to enjoy the classic favourites and seasonal specials. "Lots of our customers have become friends over the years", says Nick, who is on first-name terms with many of the regulars.

With such a warm welcome by Diane, a relaxed atmosphere and exemplary cooking, this established gem is the epitome of fine dining without the fuss.

Scutchers
So much more than just a restaurant...
Scutchers
Takeaway
Scutchers
Hog Roas
Scutchers
Restaurant
Scutchers
Restaurant

Scutchers
FILLET OF WILD TURBOT

with asparagus, broad beans, bacon and a tomato and chive dressing

One of the most popular fish dishes with the regular diners at Scutchers, turbot never fails to impress. Served up with salty bacon, fresh asparagus, broad beans and a light and refreshing dressing, this irresistible recipe is a celebration of colour and flavour on the plate. Serves 4.

Ingredients

2 large tomatoes

A bunch of asparagus, woody ends snapped off

4 x 180g turbot fillets, skinned, plus 8 small fingers of turbot

Plain flour, for coating

1 egg, beaten

Panko breadcrumbs, for coating

2 tbsp lemon juice

8 tbsp olive oil

A pinch of sugar

100g broad beans, blanched and skins removed

4 rashers unsmoked streaky bacon, cooked and cut into strips (optional)

A few chives, snipped

Oil, for deep-frying

Salt and black pepper

Method

Blanch the tomatoes in boiling water for 20 seconds, then plunge them into cold water. Remove the skins, which should now come away easily, and cut the tomatoes into quarters. Remove and discard the seeds and cut the flesh into a small dice. Set aside.

Cook the asparagus in a pan of salted boiling water for 3-4 minutes, then refresh in cold water. Set aside.

Preheat the grill to high.

Place the turbot fillets on a buttered baking tray and season with salt and pepper. Grill the turbot under the preheated grill for 5-7 minutes, until cooked through (depending on the thickness of the fish).

Place a little flour in one bowl, the beaten egg in a second bowl and the breadcrumbs in a third bowl. Dip the four fingers of turbot first in the flour, then the egg and finally the breadcrumbs. Heat the oil in a heavy-bottomed pan or deep-fryer.

Mix the lemon juice, olive oil and sugar together and season with salt and pepper to make a dressing. When the turbot is cooked, warm the dressing in a pan with the asparagus, broad beans, bacon, tomatoes and chives.

Deep-fry the turbot fingers in the hot oil, until golden and cooked through. Drain on kitchen roll.

Spoon the dressing mixture on to serving plates, place the turbot fillets on top and then add two turbot deep-fried fingers on top of each portion.

Modern COUNTRY DINING

For contemporary restaurant food served against the rural backdrop of beautiful Suffolk countryside, The Shepherd and Dog ticks all the boxes.

When Lizzie's mum told her that their local pub was up for sale, she and Greig just had to come and have a look. Having grown up in the area, Lizzie had fond memories of The Shepherd and Dog and they immediately saw huge potential in the Suffolk countryside premises. Before they knew it, it was theirs, and she and Greig were injecting their personalities and new life into the old bar and eatery.

Chef Greig Young grew up in Oban on the West coast of Scotland. With years of experience working as a chef in Michelin-starred and three AA Rosette level kitchens in the UK, he has also done stints in some world-famous Australian and New Zealand restaurants. Add to that Lizzie's background in 5-star hotels, and it's clear that this enthusiastic couple had the skills and passion to bring something new to this quiet corner of rural Suffolk.

The idea was to aim for the best modern cooking but to serve it in a relaxed environment, and to provide something a little bit different to the region. Of course you can opt to sit in the restaurant area and savour a three-course meal over a bottle of fine wine for a special evening, but you are just as welcome to choose from the same menu and eat it in the bar. Whether it's a quick snack or an evening meal, you'll be treated to the same level of fine ingredients, creative cooking and beautiful presentation.

Spoilt for choice nearby when it comes to produce, they are members of the Sustainable Restaurant Association, as well as Tastes of Anglia, which promotes the food and drink of the region. It goes without saying that everything is as local as possible on their menus. Sometimes that means it's travelled just a few miles down the road and starting this year they have planted a little kitchen garden so quite often it means it was picked shortly before being placed on the plate.

After just two years here, Lizzie and Greig have wowed visitors with their fresh approach to modern restaurant dining, gained a horde of regulars and made a permanent mark on the Suffolk culinary landscape.

GIN
is
LIQUID
SANITY
THE SHEPHERD & DOG
FRY'S COCOA
& ATE
WOODFORDE'S

The Shepherd & Dog

CRAB & CAULIFLOWER

This recipe is from one of our most talked about dishes. It is so simple to make and we love it because it conjures up those warm, homely feelings. The base of the dish always stays the same with the velvety creamed cauliflower from Cambridge and simply dressed sweet white Cromer crab meat. I recommend starting off with the best cauliflower you can find, it should be firm, with large tightly bunched florets with clean white colour and free from any holes or blemishes. When the garden is in bloom I top with peppery flowers and leaves such as nasturtium and baby rocket. Don't be afraid to change it to what's looking good in your garden at the time. Why not try watercress or the wild fennel you see dotted all over the Suffolk countryside. I hope you enjoy trying one of my personal favourites and possibly my first 'signature dish'. Serves 4.

Ingredients

1 cauliflower

100ml double cream

1 shallot, finely diced

30g butter

25ml white wine

100g picked white crab meat

2 tbsp chopped fresh chives

Grated zest of half a lemon

Nasturtium, baby rocket or samphire, to serve

Method

Remove the large florets from the cauliflower, reserving the stalks. Reserve the nicest firmest floret for slicing later and set it aside. Chop the remaining florets in to rice-sized pieces – you can use a blender but I really do prefer to do it by hand, as it retains much more texture. Set aside.

Next, make a cauliflower purée. Roughly chop the cauliflower stalks and bring to the boil in a pan of lightly salted water. Strain and repeat – this will help remove any bitterness from the stalks and give a silky-smooth texture to the purée. After straining off the second time, pour the cream over the cauliflower and bring to the boil one final time. Carefully pour the mixture into a blender and blend until smooth. Reserve until needed.

We serve raw and dried cauliflower with the dish, as it gives great textural variety. This is easiest to do on a mandoline but a sharp knife will do just fine. Slice the reserved cauliflower floret as thin as you can. Reserve half of the slices in cold water and dry the remaining half in a warm oven or warm place on a cooling rack until crisp. (This may take up to 24 hours, but if it is taking too long place in the oven at 160°C with the fan off until golden.)

Cook the diced shallot gently in the butter until soft but with no colour. Add the chopped cauliflower and continue to cook for a further 3 minutes. Add the wine and reduce.

Add half the cauliflower purée and cook the chopped cauliflower until tender. This should take approximately 4 minutes, but be sure to keep stirring and keep an eye on it. When you are happy the cauliflower is tender and the mix has thickened to a risotto-like consistency, add half the crab, 1 tbsp of the chives and season to taste.

Mix the remaining crab with the lemon zest and remaining chives. Share the cooked cauliflower cream between four hot plates or bowls. Place the dressed remaining crab meat on top. Decorate with nasturtium leaves and rocket flowers or samphire. Finally add the raw sliced cauliflower and top with the crispy dried cauliflower.

Perfect COUNTRY PUB

It's not often a pub achieves the perfect balance between traditional country pub and top-class dining destination, but the Sibton White Horse is a paragon of unpretentious culinary excellence.

Tucked away in the tranquil Suffolk countryside, the village of Sibton is a hidden treasure. Amongst its pretty Tudor timber-frame buildings stands the Sibton White Horse, loved by regulars as a friendly village local at the time as being lauded by guide books and restaurant reviewers.

Neil and Gill Mason are the charming husband and wife team behind the success. Their story here began in 2005 when they left their life in Leicestershire behind and arrived in Sibton with their son, Luke. Moving from careers in graphic design and the dental industry respectively, taking on the tired Sibton White Horse was an ambitious project.

With no experience in the industry, the transformation they achieved is incredible. Their boundless enthusiasm and passion for the pub won the hearts of the public and adulation of many a tourist guide. With awards for food and accommodation racking up year after year – including an AA rosette four years in a row, Good Pub Guide Suffolk Dining Pub of the Year 2015 and again for 2016, plus a Trip Advisor Certificate of Excellence – they have transformed the pub into a village local with a difference.

The welcome is always a warm one, whether it's a quiet drink, a three-course dinner or an overnight stay, thanks to the friendly hosts. Review after review praises the hospitality on offer here.

The seasonally changing menu celebrates the bounty of the land and sea, all skillfully prepared on-site and presented with understated elegance. The kitchen garden supplies the herbs, salad and vegetables; the meat is selected from local farms; the fish is fresh from the North Sea; and, when in season, game comes straight from the village shoot. The talented chefs embrace all aspects of cooking, making everything by hand from stocks and bread to pastries and ice cream. Keeping it simple and executing it perfectly is the secret to success.

It's not just the food and hospitality that score highly; the pub dates back to the 1500s and is riddled with original character, imposing inglenooks, old stone floors and large timber beams. Outside is equally special; there is a secluded Mediterranean-styled courtyard with the most charming sheltered dining terrace. A fabulous haven of colour during the summer, the gardens must be the White Horse's next award.

SIBTON
FREE HOUSE
ADNAMS
WHITES
Sauvignon Blanc
2·90 - 3·95 - 5·65
Chardonnay - Australia
3·15 - 4·50 - 6·30
Pinot Grigio - Italy
3·40 - 4·70 - 6·70
REDS
Merlot - Chile
2·90 - 3·95 - 5·65
Malbec - Argentina
3·15 - 4·50 - 6·30
Shiraz - Australia
3·40 - 4·70 - 6·70
ROSE - Merlot
2·90 - 3·95 - 5·65
SIBTON
WHITE HORSE

Sibton White Horse Inn

LAMB BELLY

stuffed with lamb mince and apricots

An underrated cut, lamb belly is delicious when slow-cooked to tender perfection. Cook the lamb the day before, then it simply needs to be cooked for 15 minutes before serving with luxurious fondant potatoes, home-made mint sauce, fresh vegetables and a sweet apricot purée. Serves 2.

Ingredients

For the stuffed lamb:

1 lamb belly, about 500/600g

A pinch of salt

A pinch of pepper

150g lamb mince

200g dried apricots

For the fondant potatoes:

2 potatoes, peeled

25g butter

1 vegetable stock cube

For the apricot purée:

75g dried apricots

For the mint sauce:

2 tsp water

4 tsp sugar

4 tsp malt vinegar

2 tsp chopped mint

For the vegetables:

2 pak choi

1 large courgette, sliced

Salt (optional)

Method

Preheat the oven to 200°C (fan 180°C).

Trim off any excess fat from the lamb and lay it flat. Add a pinch of salt and pepper to the minced lamb and thoroughly mix. Spread the mince evenly over one side of the lamb belly and add a line of apricots down the centre. Roll the lamb belly up tightly and tie it securely with string. Place the lamb into a deep roasting pan, add water to cover the lamb completely and cover with foil. Place in the preheated oven and cook for approximately 4 hours until tender. Allow the lamb to cool and store overnight, covered, in the fridge.

The following day, when ready to serve, preheat the oven to 200°C (fan 180°C) and allow the lamb to come back to room temperature.

For the fondant potato, cut each potato into a cylinder with a flat bottom and top, approximately 2.5cm thick. Heat the butter in a frying pan and pan-fry the potatoes in the butter over a medium heat until golden on both flat sides. Place the potato in a pan of water with the vegetable stock cube and cook in the oven for about 40 minutes until tender.

Meanwhile, prepare the apricot purée, mint sauce and lamb. For the apricot purée, place the apricots in a pan of water and bring to a simmer. Cook over a low heat for about 10-15 minutes until soft. Drain the softened apricots and blitz them in a food processor or blender until smooth.

For the mint sauce, boil the water with the sugar in a small pan for 1 minute, then add the vinegar and mint and stir thoroughly. Allow to cool. This is now ready to serve.

Heat a little oil in an ovenproof frying pan and pan-fry the lamb until it is coloured on all sides. Add a ladleful of water and put it into the oven for 15 minutes.

Cook the vegetables in boiling water until tender, adding a little salt if preferred. Trim the ends of the lamb and slice for serving. Serve with the fondant potato, apricot purée, vegetables and mint sauce.

Stay and Dine IN STYLE

Situated in 300 acres of undulating Constable Country, Stoke by Nayland Hotel, Golf & Spa not only offers secluded tranquillity, magnificent views and two championship golf courses, but it is also home to the fantastic two AA Rosette Lakes Restaurant.

It's hard to believe that this impressive hotel complex started life as a 120-acre apple farm in the 1930s. With acres of stunning rolling countryside that was unsuitable for farming, Bill and Devora Peake decided to create the Stoke by Nayland Golf Club on the site in 1972.

Since 1999 the next generation of the family have substantially expanded the original golf club, achieving an impressive resort that is home to an 80 bedroom AA 4-star hotel, five luxurious country lodges, a celebrated two AA Rosette restaurant, two stunning championship golf courses, a state-of-the-art spa and much more.

The family have kept nature and conservation at the heart of their business. The striking beauty of the area, which attracts tourists to the region year after year, can be enjoyed whether you're playing golf, fishing or enjoying afternoon tea on the terrace. The Peakes have planted over 60,000 trees on the site to date, and it's testament to this dedication to conservation that the area became an Area of Outstanding Natural Beauty after the golf courses were developed.

The farming business, Boxford Suffolk Farms, which won the national Top Fruit Grower of the Year award this year, is still one of the region's biggest producers of fruits, including apples, cherries, strawberries, raspberries and blueberries, as well as seasonal asparagus. The Morello cherries are especially celebrated, and they are used to create wonderful desserts in the award-winning restaurant.

Under the direction of executive head chef Alan Paton, the renowned restaurant is the jewel in the crown here. The menu is innovative and exciting – modern British cuisine at its best. Unusual and intriguing ingredient combinations are put together with creative flair, pushing boundaries and receiving acclaim from reviewers. Ingredients from the farm are put at the heart of dishes, and since the farm is adjacent to the hotel, they couldn't be any fresher.

Executive head chef Alan Paton has won numerous awards and is an advocate of inventive cooking and inspiring young chefs. His menus always have a magical twist that will leave diners excited and inspired. Even the bread basket will intrigue the taste buds with freshly baked options such as black olive and walnut, bacon and smoked chilli jam or blue cheese and white chocolate. If that isn't enough, the smoked bacon jam, sweet potato and pecan slaw, mint crystals and celeriac tortilla chips will certainly get guests talking!

The focus on freshness extends beyond the family's own fruits and the menu is based around the finest quality fresh ingredients sourced as close to home as possible. Meat comes from local family butchers as well as award-winning butchers, each using acclaimed farmers who put animal husbandry and care above all else. Alan Paton is particularly famous for his development of pork recipes, which are therefore extremely popular on the menu.

The restaurant is hosting a series of Foodie Nights, which all have different taster menus and accompanying wines. The series kicked off in August 2015 with Masterchef's Gregg Wallace hosting an enormously successful Foodie Night. Introducing the dishes, chatting to all the guests and hosting a question and answer session, it seems Gregg Wallace enjoyed his evening at The Lakes Restaurant as much as the guests did. Speaking after the event he said, "I thoroughly enjoyed my evening at Stoke by Nayland. It's a hotel that manages to combine style and warmth through serious professionalism."

After such a successful fun-filled evening, the next ones will be sure to sell out quickly – watch out for Jewels of the Sea, The Best of East Anglia and German Christmas Market before 2015 is over, and there will certainly be plenty more exciting events in the pipeline for 2016.

Stoke by Nayland Hotel

PARINI

Stoke by Nayland
CONFIT PORK BELLY

and pan-fried mackerel fillet with carrot buttercream, candied bacon almonds, gin-spiked blueberries, marzipan and pork jus

This is a very nicely balanced dish using blueberries from our own fruit farm in Boxford. The intriguing mix of savoury and sweet flavours marry together with exceptional results. Serves 4.

Ingredients

2 mackerel fillets, bones removed, cut from top to bottom down the middle

2 thin slices of marzipan, dried out and sliced into thin strips

Spinach, wilted in butter, to serve

Pork jus, to serve

For the pork:

800g piece of pork belly, skinned and boned

2 tbsp Maldon sea salt

½ tbsp onion powder

1 tbsp fennel seeds

A small pinch of chilli flakes

1 tsp smoked paprika

1kg duck fat

For the blueberries:

1 punnet of blueberries

25ml gin

120g caster sugar

For the carrot buttercream:

37g egg whites

70g sugar

15ml water

112g salted butter, plus 1 tbsp butter

1 tbsp olive oil

8 carrots, peeled, trimmed and chopped into 2cm chunks

For the candied bacon almonds:

12 slices thin-cut pancetta

A handful of sliced almonds

1 tbsp demerara sugar

Method

For the pork

Sprinkle 1 tbsp of the salt on the fat-side of the meat and place it fat-side down on a stainless steel tray or in a plastic container. Combine the remaining ingredients and lightly toast them in a dry frying pan set over a medium heat for 1 minute. Allow to cool and then rub into the meat. Leave to marinate for 3 hours in the fridge.

Preheat the oven to 200°C. Seal the pork in the hot oven until coloured over. Place in a roasting pan and cover with duck fat. Reduce the oven temperature to 120°C for about 3 hours until tender. Leave the pork to cool in the fat then remove it from the fat and place it on a lined baking tray and cover with a sheet of greaseproof paper. Press it evenly with a heavy weight and place it in the fridge overnight to set.

For the blueberries

Combine all the ingredients together in a pan and cook slowly over low heat until thickened and pulpy. Allow to cool and set aside.

For the carrot buttercream

To make the carrot buttercream, start by making an Italian meringue. Place a sugar thermometer in a saucepan and heat water and 60g of the sugar over a medium-high heat. Put the egg whites in a stand mixer, set the mixer to high and beat the egg whites to stiff peaks. Once stiff, gradually add the remaining sugar to the meringue. Raise the heat under the syrup and bring it to 118°C, then remove from the heat and slowly add to the meringue mixture. Reduce the speed to medium and continue to mix until cool. Once cooled, add the 112g butter, a tablespoon at a time, beating until fully incorporated. Set aside.

Now, make a carrot purée – this could be made the day before or early in the day. I personally use a pressure cooker for making this. Melt the 1 tbsp butter with the oil, add the carrots and toss over medium-high heat for 2 minutes. Cover with cold water, cover with the lid and cook over for 30 minutes. Remove from the heat, then, after 3 minutes, carefully and using a cloth, remove the pressure valve. Remove the lid and place the carrots with a little of the juice into a food processor and blitz until very smooth, adding a little more carrot liquor if required. Pass this through a sieve, and then fold into the meringue in three stages until incorporated and well mixed. Warm through over a low heat to combine completely.

For the candied bacon almonds

Preheat the oven to 160°C. Cook the pancetta in a frying pan until very crispy. Remove the pancetta and reserve the fat. When cool, crunch the pancetta up or use a food processor. Set aside. Toss the sliced almonds and demerara sugar together with the reserved fat and bake in the preheated oven for 7-10 minutes until golden. Toss in the bacon and set aside.

To plate up

Warm four plates. Remove the pork from its press and trim any rough edges (chef's snack!), then cut into four equal slices or squares – your choice. In a medium-hot non-stick pan add the pork and cook all over till golden. Remove and keep warm. Warm through the carrot. Heat through some pork jus. Place the pork pan back on the heat and cook the mackerel in it skin-side down until half cooked half way, then turn the mackerel over, remove the pan from the heat and keep warm. Place the carrot on the plate, add the pork, then the wilted spinach. Place the almonds and the marzipan on the mackerel, now place on the plate. Add the blueberries and the pork jus.

Stoke by Nayland
GLAZED CHERRIES

with cherry mousse, pistachio cake, black cherry sorbet and dried pistachio oil

We use our own grown Morello cherries from our farm in Boxford for this utterly beautiful recipe – a celebration of the wonderful English fruit. Serves 4.

Ingredients

For the glazed cherries:

200g cherries, pitted

50g sugar

For the cherry sorbet:

300g fresh or frozen cherries, pitted

75g icing sugar

For the cherry mousse:

350ml double cream

5½ sheets of gelatine

105g caster sugar

125g cherry purée

175g egg white

For the cherry gel:

100ml cherry purée

A pinch of sugar

1g agar

For the pistachio cake:

2 eggs

60g caster sugar

50g ground almonds

60g butter, melted

20g pistachio compound (a pistachio paste, available online)

For the crystallised pistachios:

25g sugar

25g water

50g pistachios

For the dried pistachio oil:

100g malto dextrin

30g pistachio oil

To decorate (optional):

Marzipan and fresh cherries

Method

For the glazed cherries

Slowly heat the cherries and sugar in a pan over a low heat for about 7-10 minutes until the cherries are tender. Strain the cherries, reserving both the cherries and the juice. Put the juice back in the pan and cook it to reduce it to a syrup. Add the cherries back into syrup, allow to cool and then place in the fridge to chill.

For the cherry sorbet

Toss the cherries in the sugar, then place in a high-powered liquidiser or vita-prep machine and blitz until smooth. Sieve the mixture discarding any solids left in the sieve and place in an insulated freeze container with lid. Freeze overnight.

For the cherry mousse

First whisk the cream until semi stiff and set aside. Soak the gelatine in cold water for 10 minutes until softened. Remove the gelatine sheets and squeeze out the water. Place the sugar in a pan, cover with 35ml of cold water and melt slowly over a low heat. Warm the purée in a separate pan, add the squeezed gelatine sheets and mix to melt the gelatine. Allow to cool.

Turn the heat up on the sugar and cook until it reaches 121°C on a sugar thermometer. Meanwhile, whisk the eggs to soft peaks. Gradually add the sugar syrup while you continue whisking (ask someone else to help you do this, if you like) and keep whisking until the mixture has cooled.

Fold the whipped cream into the purée in three stages, then fold in the meringue. Pour into moulds and place in the freezer until set. This will take about 3 hours – they are ready when they pop cleanly out of the moulds. Allow to defrost in the fridge.

For the cherry gel

Bring the cherry purée and sugar to the boil in a small saucepan. Whisk in the agar, then allow to cool and place in the fridge to chill. Once chilled, blitz until smooth.

For the pistachio cake

Preheat the oven to 150°C (fan 130°C). Whisk the eggs and sugar together until light and fluffy. Mix the melted butter with the ground almonds and pistachio compound. Fold into the egg mixture. Pour into cake moulds of your choice (roughly 120ml in volume) and bake for 20-30 minutes depending on size of mould.

For the crystallised pistachios

Bring the water and sugar to 113°C on a sugar thermometer, pour in the nuts and keep stirring until the sugar crystallises. Place onto a baking tray to cool.

For the dried pistachio oil

Whisk the malto dextrin into the pistachio oil to make a "dried" crumbly oil which softens on the palate.

To plate up

Warm the cake through. Use a palette knife to spread the gel on the plate. Use a piping bag to dress extra gel onto the plate. Place the warmed cake across the gel. Add the dried oil and glazed cherries to the plate. Scatter the crystallised pistachios across the plate. Quenelle the sorbet and place on. Decorate with a circle of blow-torched marzipan and fresh cherries, if you like.

A herd of award-winning Guernsey cows, three artisan cheeses and an innovative milk vending machine – Suffolk Farmhouse Cheeses are bringing together traditional farming methods and state-of-the-art technology in a dairy-farming success story.

The art of cheese-making has remained remarkably unchanged for centuries. Making fantastic cheeses relies on craftsmanship and the finest milk, and artisan cheese-makers, Jason and Katharine Salisbury, possess both of these key ingredients for success.

First-generation farmers, Jason had experience working in the dairy industry and Katharine was a veterinary surgeon before they made the life-changing decision to follow their dream to start their own dairy herd and produce cheese. Starting a farm from scratch involved extensive research and planning, and the first few years saw them grow their herd and their business steadily.

Today, they have 80 award-winning Guernsey dairy cows, of which they have around 30 in milk at any one time, providing about 500 litres of fresh milk each day. Katharine and Jason know each of their cows by name, as well as by their distinct personalities. The health and happiness of the cows is paramount, with the herd grazing on the lush pastures throughout the summer and being cared for in the brand new cow shed during the harsh winter. With high-quality feed and top-notch care, the milk is a world away from supermarket offerings. Rich and creamy, it lends itself perfectly to being transformed into craft cheeses, which Katharine does using traditional methods and tried-and-tested recipes.

Suffolk Gold is their creamy, semi-hard farmhouse cheese. Its rich golden colour is revealed when it's cut open. For something a little more luxurious, Suffolk Blue never fails to please – soft and indulgent, its light blue veins change depending on the season, but its deep flavour remains all year round. They also make Suffolk Brie, a creamy cheese that is an ever-popular choice.

Producing 18 tonnes of cheese a year, Suffolk Farmhouse Cheeses is now a familiar sight on cheeseboards across the county. However, not all the milk is used for cheese; it is also sold on-site from the ingenious new milk vending machine. Bring a reusable container along and fill it with the delicious fresh milk. Don't worry if you forget a bottle though – you can always buy one on-site.

SUFFOLK FARMHOUSE CHEESES
Suffolk Gold
FARMHOUSE CHEESE
a specialist, luxury cheese made with the rich and creamy milk from our small herd of pedigree Guernsey cows
MADE BY HAND IN SUFFOLK IP6 8PG
WWW.SUFFOLKCHEESE.CO.UK

Suffolk Farmhouse Cheeses

SUFFOLK GOLD RAREBIT

with caramelised red onions

This is a very simple recipe for "posh cheese on toast", making the most of the rich golden colour of the cheese and natural sweetness of the onions. Delicious! If you do not have time to prepare the caramelised onions, a red onion marmalade is a good substitute. Serves 4.

Ingredients

225g Suffolk Gold from Suffolk Farmhouse Cheeses, grated (tip – grate it straight out of the fridge)

25g butter

1 tsp English mustard powder

4 tbsp brown ale

1 tsp Worcestershire sauce

4 slices of sourdough (or another good-quality bread)

Salt and black pepper

Fresh green salad leaves, to serve

For the caramelised onions:

2 tbsp olive oil

2 large red onions, sliced

1 tsp salt

1 tbsp caster sugar

1 tbsp balsamic vinegar

Method

Start by making the caramelised onions. Put the olive oil in a wide, heavy-based sauté pan. This allows maximum pan-contact with the onions. Heat over a medium heat until the oil is shimmering, then add the sliced onions. Stir to coat in the oil, then spread evenly and let cook, stirring occasionally.

After 10 minutes, sprinkle the salt over the onions and add the sugar. Stir, lower the heat and cook for 30-60 minutes, stirring every few minutes. If the onions start drying out, add a little more oil. Allow the onions to stick a little, then stir – but be careful not to let them burn.

When the onions are a nice brown colour and have reduced, remove from the heat and add the balsamic vinegar and stir to help deglaze the pan. Alternatively, the caramelised onions can be prepared by putting all the ingredients except the vinegar in a slow cooker or low oven/aga and cooking all day until soft, dark brown and reduced. They may need stirring occasionally. Stir in the vinegar at the end.

To make the rarebit, preheat the grill.

Place the grated cheese, butter, mustard, ale and Worcestershire sauce into a heavy-based saucepan and heat very gently until a creamy mixture is obtained. Season to taste.

Lightly toast the bread on one side. Place the bread in a baking tray or grill pan toasted-side down and pour the sauce over the un-toasted side of the bread. Place under the hot grill and cook until golden and bubbling.

Serve with the caramelised onions and a fresh green salad.

Food and Farming

CHAMPIONS

When it comes to making local produce available, nowhere has been quite as ambitious as Suffolk Food Hall, and the accolades for their hard work just keep on coming...

Farming and food has always been at the heart of things here. With seven generations of the Paul family farming around Ipswich, there's nothing that these foodie pioneers don't know about local produce. Suffolk Food Hall was opened underneath the Orwell Bridge when the Paul family realised that people living nearby were finding it difficult to source local ingredients. With an abundance of fresh produce on the doorstep – daily catches of fish from the Suffolk coast, native-breed cattle and sheep that graze on the lush pastures around the estuaries, and crops that thrive on the fertile fields – the family set about an ambitious project to bring all this bountiful produce to one place.

When you arrive at Suffolk Food Hall, it's clear to see they achieved this dream and a whole lot more. The large farm shop is a celebration of Suffolk farming heritage. Every piece of pork on sale is butchered on site from their own pigs. The game is their own too, so what's available will depend on what's in season, but venison and partridge are firm favourites among their customers. Such is the demand for the pedigree beef that, along with their own Red Poll herd, they also butcher beef from other trusted local farmers. A seven-metre long wet fish counter displays a whopping variety of fish when there's been a good catch, the delicatessen showcases an unrivalled array of local produce and the scratch bakery operates seven days a week.

It's no surprise that the awards just keep on coming for these local food heroes. The Countryside Alliance Rural Oscars recently named them 'Champion of Champions' as best local food venue, comparing all the winners from the last 10 years. With awards from the national farm shop association (FARMA) and three Gold Star Great Taste awards already under their belt, Suffolk Food Hall is not only a shining example in Suffolk, but is showing the rest of the UK how it's done.

Suffolk Food Hall

Suffolk Food Hall

THE SUFFOLK SURF & TURF

'Cowboy and crab'

Pop down to The Suffolk Food Hall and grab a basketful of local produce to make this outstanding sharing platter. The crab can be prepared in advance, as it is the most time-consuming and difficult part of the recipe. Place it in the fridge until you are ready to prepare the rest of the dish. Serves 2-3 to share.

Ingredients

1 whole brown crab, about 1kg

150g butter

1 lemon

½ tsp Worcestershire sauce

A few chives, finely chopped

400g Broxtead new potatoes

1 Broxtead onion, peeled, halved and sliced

1 cowboy steak, about 600g-700g (single Côte du Boeuf/ribeye on the bone)

1 clove garlic, crushed

A sprig of rosemary

1 bag of Alison Bond's organic salad

Hill Farm rapeseed oil

Maldon sea salt and black pepper

Method

Begin by preparing the crab. Place the crab into a pan of boiling salted water. Boil for 30 minutes per kg. Remove the crab once cooked and set aside to cool.

Once cool, you need to prepare the crab in three different ways and then set aside. Begin by removing the claws and legs. Crack the legs open and remove all of the white crab flesh. Carefully pick through this to remove and discard any shell.

Crack the claws gently and remove each claw as one whole piece. You may need to snap the small pincer.

Finally you need to remove the brown meat from the shell. Carefully remove the soft under-shell and discard the dead man's fingers. Scrape out all of the brown meat.

Chop the brown meat until a paste is created. Mix this with 100g of the butter, the Worcestershire sauce and chopped chives. Grate in the zest of the lemon, then cut it in half and add the juice of one half. Set aside the other lemon half for later. Mix and season well.

Set aside the three elements of prepared crab while you prepare the rest of the dish. If you are not preparing the meal immediately, place the crab in the fridge. Alternatively, order a dressed one from Suffolk Food Hall!

Preheat the oven to 180°C (fan 160°C).

Next, prepare the potatoes. Cut the potatoes into halves or quarters, depending on their size. Season well and generously coat in rapeseed oil. Spread the potatoes evenly onto a baking tray in one layer and place in the preheated oven for about 10 minutes.

Meanwhile, add the sliced onion to a hot frying pan with 1 tablespoon rapeseed oil and start to fry gently. After about 10 minutes the onion should be soft and golden brown. At this point, remove the potatoes from the oven and sprinkle the onions over the top. Return the baking tray to the oven.

When the potatoes are in the oven and the crab prepared, it is time to cook the steak. Heat an ovenproof chargrill pan or frying pan over a high heat until almost smoking and add a little rapeseed oil. Season the steak, place into the hot pan and cook on both sides until golden brown.

Add the remaining butter, crushed garlic clove and rosemary to the pan. Baste the steak with the butter, then place the pan in the oven. Cook the steak to your choosing, around 6-8 minutes for medium. Add the crab claws for the last 5 minutes to warm through. Set the steak and crab claws aside to rest whilst constructing the rest of the dish.

Mix the washed salad leaves with the white crab meat and dress with a drizzle of rapeseed oil and a squeeze of lemon juice from the reserved half. Place on a large platter.

Take the potatoes out of the oven; they should be golden brown with crunchy, crispy onions. Place in a bowl and add to the serving platter.

Baste the steak one last time and then slice into strips across the grain of the meat. Add to the platter. Set the claws to the side of it and finish by serving a generous scoop of the crab butter on top of the hot steak, so that it begins to melt and creates a sauce.

What's the HOO HA?

Remember when chicken used to taste of, well, chicken? Charles and Belinda Nash set about bringing truly free-range chickens back into our hearts and onto our tables with their award-winning Sutton Hoo Chicken.

Charles and Belinda were farmers on a mission. Passionate about poultry, they set about rearing a traditional slow-growing breed of chicken in the Suffolk countryside they call home. Their commitment was to give their chickens the highest welfare possible, to avoid all additives and antibiotics and to go over and above the accepted idea of 'free-range' to something truly remarkable.

Their 40 acres of meadow, over which the birds roam freely, overlooks the River Deben in the Sutton Hoo grasslands. Happy chicks graze naturally, pecking in the fields and foraging in the vegetation. Mobile open housing provides shelter – naturally ventilated with no artificial lighting of course. It's no wonder Charles and Belinda took such joy in seeing their dreams come to life as they watched their poultry thrive under their traditional husbandry.

Sadly, Charles Nash, known by all around him for his cheerful disposition, impassioned love of the Suffolk countryside and ardent support of real food, passed away suddenly at the age of 48. Leaving such a legacy of success in his development of Sutton Hoo Chicken, his wife Belinda took over the reins and has continued to see their family business thrive in his memory.

Chefs all over the country rely on Sutton Hoo Chicken for getting the best flavour possible, while being reassured that their chickens were reared to the highest animal welfare standards. In fact, the two qualities are intrinsically linked – only by committing to rearing the right breed in the right way with the right care can you achieve the best flavour. As Belinda explains: "It is because our chickens have more exercise, are grown for longer and have a natural, varied diet that they taste so much better."

Sutton Hoo Chicken have never altered their standard of what it means to be free-range, which means going over and above all other expectations. And that's the way they plan to continue – reminding us that food tastes better when it is produced slowly with love and care.

Sutton Hoo Chicken

AUTUMN ONE-PAN ROAST

The flavour of a truly free-range chicken that has been slow-reared is best experienced in a simple whole roast chicken recipe. This is a classic family recipe that everyone will enjoying sharing. Serves 4-6.

Ingredients

125g butter, softened

1 whole free-range Sutton Hoo chicken (about 1.8kg), patted dry with absorbent paper

4 large carrots, peeled and cut into chunks

2 large potatoes, peeled and cut into large wedges

1 red onion, peeled and cut into large wedges

½ bunch thyme or rosemary

150ml olive oil

4 whole cooked beetroot, peeled and cut into chunks

200g spinach, thoroughly washed and drained

Salt and black pepper

Fresh bread, to serve (optional)

Method

Preheat the oven to 230°C (fan 210°C).

Smear the butter all over the chicken and season well with salt and pepper inside and out.

Take a large wide-bottomed pan and spread the carrots, potatoes and red onion over the bottom of the pan. Season with salt and pepper and scatter with the herbs. Pour over the oil and mix well.

Place the whole chicken on top of the vegetables and put into the preheated oven. Turn the oven down to 200°C (fan 180°C) after 10 minutes. Roast for 45 minutes, then remove from the oven and carefully mix in the beetroot and spinach and take the opportunity to baste the chicken. Place back in the oven to cook for a further 10 minutes. The skin should be crispy and golden in colour. Check the chicken is cooked through by piercing the thickest part of the thigh with a skewer and checking the juices are clear.

Remove from the oven and leave to rest in a warm place for 15 minutes, loosely covered with foil.

Place the whole pan in the middle of the dining table to share between everyone. There will be some delicious juices in the pan so we recommend mixing these well with the vegetables and serving with bread to mop then up. So tasty!

Creative British and European cooking at affordable prices, The Townhouse Restaurant is a shining example of modern fine dining.

With its name taken from the attractive building in which it is housed, this popular local restaurant is a gem in the heart of Ipswich town centre.

Whether they're relaxing with a cup of coffee in the afternoon, enjoying a glass of wine in the cosy bar, sampling one of the excellent value lunch options or treating themselves to an evening dinner in the charming restaurant, guests at The Townhouse Restaurant will be met with a welcoming smile and dedicated service.

Set over three floors, a lot of thought has been put into the beautiful interior, which meticulously balances a relaxing atmosphere with high-end attention to detail. The exposed brickworks, stunning beams and vaulted ceilings create a light and airy atmosphere on the top floor, while there are cosy corners in the bar to enjoy a glass or two from the extensive wine list.

In the kitchen, it's head chef Jason Dinverno who is responsible for putting this local treasure on the food-lover's map. His imaginative approach to cooking and flair for flavour combinations can be seen on the restaurant's menus – intriguing examples include pigeon breast with mushrooms, bacon and blackberries or deconstructed beef Wellington with potato scone, buttered spinach and Madeira jus.

And there's no reason to stop there. The dessert list here is just as creative – a gin and tonic granita with chilled cucumber is ideal to bring the meal to an irresistibly refreshing finish.

As well as the impressive à la carte menu, diners can also indulge in the two or three-course set menus. With more than 30 wines on offer by the glass and knowledgeable staff on hand to help you choose, one thing is for sure – you will always find the perfect pairing to complement your meal.

Prosecco
the townhouse
restaurant
01473 2

The Townhouse FILLET STEAK

with Cashel Blue cheese and wilted spinach on a herbed rösti

For an impressive dish to serve at a dinner party, look no further than this luxurious combination from The Townhouse's chef, Jason. The combination of rich blue cheese with fresh wilted spinach is a real winner, and the classic rösti is made extra-special with a herby hit. Serves 4.

Ingredients

For the herbed rösti:

4 medium potatoes, peeled

1 small onion, finely chopped

60g butter, softened

2 tbsp chopped fresh mixed herbs (such as rosemary, thyme and parsley), plus extra herbs to garnish

2 tbsp vegetable oil

Salt and black pepper

For the steaks:

4 x 170g fillet steaks

2 tbsp vegetable oil

160g Cashel Blue cheese, cut into 4 slices

Salt and black pepper

For the red wine jus:

200ml red wine

50g chilled butter, cubed

1 medium tomato, peeled, deseeded and finely diced

1 tbsp finely chopped shallots, sautéed until softened

Salt and black pepper

For the wilted spinach:

A knob of butter

200g baby spinach

Salt and black pepper

Method

Coarsely grate the potatoes and squeeze out the excess water. Place the grated potato in a mixing bowl with the chopped onion, butter and chopped fresh herbs. Season with salt and pepper and mix together. Divide the rösti mixture into four equal portions. Use ring moulds to shape the röstis into perfect circles or shape them by hand.

Heat the oil in a non-stick frying pan. Add the röstis and cook for 10 minutes over a medium heat until golden and crisp on the bottom, and then turn over and cook for a further 10 minutes.

Meanwhile, season the steaks with salt and pepper. Heat the oil in a frying pan or griddle pan over a high heat and cook the steaks to your liking. Remove the steaks and set aside to rest.

Add 2 tbsp water to the pan and scrape with a wooden spoon to deglaze. Pour the deglazing juices into a saucepan for the red wine jus. Place the saucepan over a high heat, add the red wine and bring to the boil, then reduce the heat to low and simmer, uncovered, until the sauce has reduced by half. Add the chilled, cubed butter a piece at a time, whisking gently, to make a buttery sauce. Season to taste, add the diced tomatoes and shallots, keep warm until required.

Preheat a grill to high, ready to finish off the steaks.

For the spinach, melt the butter in a pan, add the spinach and cook for 1 minute, stirring until wilted.

To serve, put a slice of Cashel Blue cheese on top of each steak and place under the preheated grill to melt. Place a rösti on each plate and top with spinach. Place a cheese-topped steak on top of each portion and drizzle a little jus around the plate. Garnish with some fresh herbs.

A Taste of SPAIN

Situated above Baileys delicatessen, which has been a mainstay of Beccles life for many years, Upstairs at Baileys is impressing diners with authentic Spanish flavours and modern Mediterranean cooking.

Nestled in the picturesque streets of the market town of Beccles, Baileys prides itself on being a true food-lover's paradise. Downstairs it houses a delicatessen that is sure to delight lovers of cured meats – English ham, Italian salami and Spanish chorizo and Serrano are amongst the selection of international specialities on offer. Over 50 fine cheeses from around the world are available and there is an array of chutneys and preserves to accompany them.

Make your way through the mouthwatering delicatessen and up the stairs and you'll be welcomed into the bright restaurant, Upstairs at Baileys. Offering a set lunch menu that changes daily, this is the perfect place to enjoy a relaxing three-course midday meal.

On Friday and Saturday evenings, the restaurant transforms into a fine-dining establishment offering authentic and exciting Spanish dishes. Head chef Mauro Rodriguez has brought his talent and passion for modern and inventive Mediterranean food to the eatery and his dishes are certainly wowing the locals.

Starters include octopus with quinoa and chorizo velouté and black spaghetti with lobster Bolognese and fresh crab bisque, showcasing his flair for bringing together traditional cooking techniques and contemporary flavour combinations. As for main courses, the options are impressive and perfectly executed, with such delights as Catalan black rice with monkfish, cuttlefish and oyster mushrooms on offer.

A meal isn't complete without a dessert, and whether you're looking for something rich and indulgent (think coffee mousse with lime gel, Amaretto cream, Muscovado crumble and milk ice cream) or something light and refreshing (such as elderflower gin and tonic with Granny Smith sorbet), dinner always ends with something sophisticated and elegant.

The staff are on hand to offer expert advice on the wines to accompany your dinner, or you can choose one from the deli downstairs to enjoy with your meal. With creative cooking, extensive wine lists and impressive service, Upstairs at Baileys has succeeded in bringing modern Mediterranean dining to this quaint English market town.

UPSTAIRS at BAILEYS

Upstairs at Baileys

APPLE & BLACK PUDDING RAVIOLI

with cheese crème

You will need half-sphere silicon moulds to shape these beautiful ravioli. Instead of pasta, delicate slices of apple encase a luscious black pudding filling. Serves 4.

Ingredients

100g sugar

100ml water

2 apples

400g black pudding, warmed

200ml double cream

100g Parmesan cheese, freshly grated

Salt and black pepper

Method

Mix the sugar and water in a saucepan and place over the heat to cook until the sugar has melted completely. Remove the pan from the heat and set aside.

Slice the apples thinly, about 2mm thick. As soon as you have sliced the apples, dip them into the sugar syrup to stop them from discolouring.

Take a half-sphere silicon ravioli mould and use some of the apple slices to line 12 of the hollows. Fill the moulds with warm black pudding and finish by covering the moulds with more apple slices to encase the black pudding. Place the moulds in the fridge.

Place the cream in a saucepan and heat over a medium heat until it starts to boil, then remove the pan from the heat and add the grated cheese. Stir until it melts and season with salt and pepper to taste.

Carefully remove the ravioli from the moulds and quickly heat them up in the microwave.

Put some cheese crème on each serving plate and arrange three ravioli on each portion. Garnish with some edible petals, flowers and micro herbs.

Happy SHOPPING

Willow Tree Farm Shop is more than a place for people to buy fresh Suffolk produce; it's a community hub where people come to enjoy shopping the old-fashioned way.

There's a certain buzz around this thriving fine foods store. Loyal customers began coming here to buy the freshest vegetables straight from the ground, but today there's a lot more to this family business than meets the eye.

Matthew is the third generation of the Russell family to begin making his mark on Willow Tree Farm, along with his parents Deborah and Michael. Bought by Michael's father in the 1950s when he returned to Suffolk after a few years of farming in Canada, this charming plot was once a poultry and egg farm. It was Michael (who can usually be spotted weeding, digging and picking in the fields) who decided to start selling fresh produce from the gate.

Today, it's a booming business with mum Deborah, who is usually found with a grandchild under one arm and an ordering pad under the other, managing everything behind the scenes. Not only are they selling home-grown vegetables and freshly laid eggs, but a plethora of fine foods from local suppliers too.

Tempting goodies include artisan breads, gluten-free loaves, fresh pies and a huge range of cheeses. Store-cupboard essentials are all on sale too, from locally made chutneys and jams to carefully selected spice kits and more unusual Asian condiments. As keen cooks, the Russell family have tried and tested it all and will happily make recommendations!

It's not just the impressive array of products on offer that has their customers coming back time and time again – some of them have been shopping here for 30 years. It's the extra touches that made this such a beloved part of Glemsford life. There's no rush here; there's always time for a catch up at the till. They know most of their customers by their first names. They'll deliver to people free of charge, help to carry bags to the car and make shopping a relaxed and friendly experience.

"We like to think we've captured the way shopping used to be", says Matthew, "this is a hub of the community where people can catch up with friends, share recipe ideas and enjoy a slower pace of life."

Willow Tree
Farm Shop

Willow Tree Farm Shop

SUMMER ROASTED VEGETABLE PASTA SAUCE

This is an economical, healthy and satisfying meal. It costs only about £2.20 per head to whip up, but is also great for using up surplus vegetables from the garden and can be easily adapted to suit your taste. Don't fancy the veggie option? Why not try cooking chicken breasts in the finished sauce. Serves 4.

Ingredients

For the sauce:

2 medium red onions, roughly chopped

3 cloves garlic, finely chopped

1 large carrot, cubed

1 large courgette, cubed

1 red pepper, cubed

4 ripe tomatoes, quartered

1 red chilli, finely chopped (optional)

2 bay leaves

2 tbsp Suffolk rapeseed oil

2 tbsp Suffolk runny honey

2 tbsp Suffolk balsamic vinegar

400g tin of chopped tomatoes

A good handful of fresh basil, roughly torn

Flaked sea salt and freshly ground pepper

To serve:

500g penne pasta

Parmigiano Reggiano cheese (the proper stuff is our favourite, but substitute vegetarian Italian-style hard cheese if serving to vegetarians)

A handful of fresh basil leaves

Method

Preheat the oven to 200°C (180°C fan) and warm some pasta bowls.

Scatter the prepared vegetables (onion, garlic, carrot, courgette, pepper, tomatoes and chilli) in a large roasting tin along with the bay leaves and coat with the rapeseed oil. Roast in the preheated oven for 15 minutes.

Meanwhile, bring a pan of salted water to the boil, ready for the pasta.

Remove the vegetables from the oven, drizzle over the honey and balsamic vinegar and season well with the salt and pepper. Roast for a further 10 minutes.

Meanwhile, cook the pasta in the boiling water according to the instructions on the packet. This usually this takes about 10 minutes.

Remove the roasting tin from the oven and set aside one-third of the roasted vegetables. Place the remaining mixture (including the bay leaves) into a large saucepan and add the tinned tomatoes. Bring to the boil and simmer for 2 minutes. Remove from the heat and fish out and discard the bay leaves. Blitz the sauce with a stick blender until smooth(ish).

Return the reserved roasted vegetables to the sauce along with the fresh basil. Drain the cooked pasta. Serve the pasta in warmed serving bowls with the sauce, fresh basil leaves and shavings of fresh Parmigiano Reggiano cheese. We are also partial to an extra grinding of freshly cracked black pepper before serving.

These great businesses have supported the making of this book; please support and enjoy them.

The Anchor Woodbridge
19 Quay Street, Woodbridge
Suffolk IP12 1BX
Telephone: 01394 382649
Website:
www.theanchorwoodbridge.co.uk
Traditional quayside pub serving cask ales and fresh home-made food made with locally sourced ingredients.

Bistro on the Quay
Wherry Quay, Ipswich
Suffolk IP4 1AS
Telephone: 01473 286677
Website: www.bistroonthequay.co.uk
Waterfront restaurant serving excellent food and wine in a relaxed and friendly atmosphere.

The Brewery Tap
Cliff Road, Cliff Quay, Ipswich
Suffolk IP3 0AT
Telephone: 01473 225501
Website: www.thebrewerytap.org
Pub famed for locally brewed beers, cool music, beer gardens and excellent quality food made on the premises.

The Castle Inn
35 Earsham Street, Bungay
Suffolk NR35 1AF
Telephone: 01986 892283
Website: www.thecastleinn.net
Historic inn with four bedrooms, serving Michelin-recommended and locally sourced food.

Cult Café Bar
James Hehir Building
University Avenue, Ipswich
Suffolk IP3 0FS
Telephone: 01473 338166
Website: www.cultcafe.co.uk
Waterfront café bar with live events, locally brewed beers and a globally inspired menu.

Curry with Love
Email: ordercurrywithlove@gmail.com
Website: www.curry-with-love.co.uk
Authentic spice kits hand-blended in Bury St Edmunds, available to order online.

Depden Farm Shop
Rookery Farm, Depden, Bury St Edmunds
Suffolk IP29 4BU
Telephone: 01284 852525
Website: www.depden.com
Farm shop, café and training centre promoting local produce, artisan delicacies and training opportunities related to food and farming.

The Edwardstone White Horse Inn,
Mill Green, Edwardstone, Sudbury,
Suffolk CO10 5PX
Telephone: 01787 211211
Website:
www.edwardstonewhitehorse.co.uk
Eco-friendly, traditional pub with on-site brewery, campsite and two self-catering cottages, serving locally sourced food.

Elveden Farms Ltd
London Road, Elveden, Thetford
Suffolk IP24 3TQ
Restaurant: 01842 898066
Food Hall: 01842 898064
Website: www.elveden.com
Producer and purveyor of local and regional foods, with shopping, dining and accommodation in beautiful surroundings.

Emmerdale Farm Shop
Westleton Road, Darsham, Saxmundham
Suffolk IP17 3BP
Telephone: 01728 668648
Website: www.emmerdalefarmshop.co.uk
Butchery, tea room and large farm shop selling everything from vegetables, fruit and store-cupboard ingredients to frozen food, garden products, pet supplies and logs.

Friday Street Farm Shop
Friday Street, Farnham, Saxmundham, Suffolk IP17 1JX
Telephone: 01728 602783
Website: www.farmshopsuffolk.co.uk
Farm shop selling home-grown vegetables and local produce, as well as butchery, strawberry picking, café restaurant and home store.

The Great House
Market place, Lavenham
Suffolk CO10 9QZ
Telephone: 01787 247431
Website: www.greathouse.co.uk
Award-winning French cuisine in an English country boutique guest house.

Gressingham Foods
Loomswood Farm, Debach, Woodbridge
Suffolk IP13 6JW
Switchboard: 01473 735456
Sales: 01473 734200
Website: www.gressinghamduck.co.uk
The remarkable Gressingham Duck® from Red Tractor assured farms in beautiful East Anglia, a unique breed renowned for its superior taste and higher percentage of breast meat.

Harriets Café Tearooms
57 Cornhill Buildings, Bury St Edmunds
Suffolk IP33 1BT
Telephone: 01284 756256
Website: www.harrietscafetearooms.co.uk
Traditional tearooms serving breakfasts, light lunches and afternoon tea in elegant surroundings. Other branches in Cambridge and Norwich.

Hodmedod Ltd
The Bean Store
Unit 8, Halesworth Business Centre, Halesworth
Suffolk IP19 8QJ
Telephone: 01986 467567
Website: www.hodmedods.co.uk
Hodmedod works with British farmers to source and provide British-grown beans, peas and quinoa.

Jimmy's Farm
Pannington Hall Lane, Ipswich
Suffolk IP9 2AR
Telephone: 01473 604206
Website: www.jimmysfarm.com
Farm with farm shop, restaurant and butchery, as well as farm park with rare-breed animals and plenty of family activities.

Maison Bleue
30/31 Churchgate Street, Bury St Edmunds
Suffolk IP33 1RG
Telephone: 01284 760623
Website: www.maisonbleue.co.uk
Award-winning and highly praised fine-dining restaurant in the medieval town of Bury St Edmunds.

Mrs Bennett's Pickles & Chutneys
Email: info@mrsbennetts.co.uk
Telephone: 01473 822650
Website: www.mrsbennetts.co.uk
A family business making a range of home-made pickles and chutneys in Polstead, Suffolk.

Munchy Seeds
6a Eastlands Road, Leiston
Suffolk IP16 4LL
Telephone: 01728 833004
Website: www.munchyseeds.co.uk
Munchy Seeds specialise in creating delicious blends of spicy, savoury and sweet roasted seed snacks.

Palfrey & Hall
The Food Hub, Kenton Hall Estate
Bellwell Lane, Debenham, Stowmarket
Suffolk, IP14 6JX
Telephone: 01728 861862
Website: www.palfreyandhall.co.uk
Bespoke cutting, curing and smoking of meats using time-honoured techniques.

The Pantry
Unit 17 and 18 The Guineas
Newmarket
Suffolk CB8 8EQ
Telephone: 01638 661181
Website: www.thepantryfinefoods.com
Fine food shop and restaurant – showcasing the best the region has to offer.

The Plough & Sail,
Snape Maltings, Snape,
Suffolk IP17 1SR
Telephone: 01728 688413
Website:
www.theploughandsailsnape.com
Country dining pub offering relaxed lunches and formal dining, as well as an outdoor terrace.

Red Chilli Kitchen
Saxmundham Road, Aldeburgh
Suffolk IP15 5PB
Website: www.redchillikitchen.co.uk
Email: sales@redchillikitchen.co.uk
Telephone: 07977 219169
Delicious range of authentic Vietnamese products, including curry paste, tomato marinade, miracle dressing and marinade, and award-winning tomato chilli jam.

Salubrious Sauce Company
Telephone: 01394 446028
Website: www.salubrioussauceco.co.uk
Email: monty@salubrioussauceco.co.uk
Home of the original British Breakfast Sauce, a unique new condiment made in Suffolk.

Scarlett & Mustard
The Dressing Room, Moat Park, Earl Soham
Suffolk, IP13 7SR
Telephone: 01728 685210
Website:
www.scarlettandmustard.co.uk
Award-winning producers of dressings, sauces, oils, savoury jams, relishes and curds.

Scutchers
Westgate Street, Long Melford, Sudbury
Suffolk CO10 9DP
Telephone: 01787 310200
Website: www.scutchers.com
Fine-dining restaurant open Thursday, Friday and Saturday for lunch and dinner. Scutchers also cater for occasions such as weddings, business events and large parties.

The Shepherd & Dog
Forward Green, Stowmarket
Suffolk IP14 5HN
Telephone: 01449 711685
Website:
www.theshepherdanddog.com
Bar, lounge and eatery with a modern restaurant menu served in relaxed surroundings.

Sibton White Horse
Halesworth Road, Sibton, Nr Saxmundham
Suffolk IP17 2JJ
Telephone: 01728 660337
Email:
info@sibtonwhitehorseinn.co.uk
Historic village inn offering award-winning food and 4-star accommodation.

Stoke by Nayland Hotel, Golf & Spa
Keepers Lane, Leavenheath
Colchester CO6 4PZ
Telephone: 01206 262836
Website: www.stokebynayland.com
Email: sales@stokebynayland.com
Award-winning family-owned resort including an 80 bedroom AA 4-star hotel, luxurious country lodges, extensive spa, two golf courses and a two AA Rosette restaurant.

Suffolk Farmhouse Cheeses
Whitegate Farm, Norwich Road, Creeting St Mary
Suffolk IP6 8PG
Telephone : 01449 710458
Website: www.suffolkcheese.co.uk
Family-run business hand-making cheeses using their own milk and traditional methods.

Suffolk Food Hall Ltd
Wherstead, Ipswich
Suffolk IP9 2AB
Food Hall: 01473 786610
Restaurant: 01473 786616
Website: www.suffolkfoodhall.co.uk
Internationally recognised farm shop with butchery, bakery, deli, wet fish counter, wine and beer merchant, green grocer, restaurant and more.

Sutton Hoo Chicken
Kennel Farm, Hasketon
Suffolk IP13 6JX
Telephone: 01394 386797
Website: www.suttonhoochicken.co.uk
Truly free-range chicken, traditionally reared and slow-grown in the Suffolk countryside.

The Table
3 Quay Street, Woodbridge
Suffolk IP12 1BX
Telephone: 01394 382428
Website:
www.thetablewoodbridge.co.uk
Relaxed brasserie-style restaurant in a delightful setting with a courtyard for outside dining.

The Townhouse Restaurant
4a Orwell Place, Ipswich
Suffolk IP4 1BB
Telephone: 01473 230254
Website:
www.thetownhouserestaurant.com
Creative English and European cooking with an unhurried and relaxed approach to dining.

Upstairs at Baileys
2 Hungate, Beccles
Suffolk NR34 9TL
Telephone: 01502 710609
Website: www.upstairsatbaileys.co.uk
Restaurant situated above the Baileys Delicatessen, serving a lunch menu Monday-Saturday and fine-dining meals on Friday and Saturday evenings.

Willow Tree Farm Shop
Lower Road, Glemsford, Sudbury
Suffolk CO10 7QU
Telephone: 01787 280341
Website:
www.willowtreefarmshop.co.uk
A family farm shop with traditional values, selling a whole host of fresh produce, fine foods, logs and store-cupboard essentials.

A.R.
12

IPSWICH A 14
STOWMARKET A 14
SUDBURY A134
A143 YARMOUTH
A1101 MILDENHALL
A134 THETFORD
Really Rather Good
COFFEE HOUSE
18 different Loose Leaf Teas
Beers & Wines • Home-made Cakes
Take
F41S
F421
FUR TH
REDUC TI
SALE